HORSE PSYCHOLOGY

MOYRA WILLIAMS

HORSE PSYCHOLOGY

J. A. ALLEN

LONDON

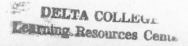

ISBN 0-85131-238-1

First published 1956
Revised and reset 1976
Revised format published 1985
Reprinted 1986, 1991

Book production Bill Ireson

Printed and bound in Great Britain by
Biddles Ltd, Guildford and King's Lynn

CONTENTS

LIST OF ILLUSTRATIONS

INTRODUCTION

THE BOOK

There are probably few words which conjure up more erroneous ideas of their meaning than that of Psychology. While to some people psychology is synonymous with sex, to others it implies only statistics and tables. While some people quake at the thought of meeting a psychologist, believing that there innermost beliefs and desires will immediately become known, others think that after having read one or two books by Freud they are psychologists themselves.

None of these attitudes is wholly justified. Psychology is more than sex and statistics, but it is neither myth nor magic. It is a subject and a method. Its subject is the study of mental activity and its method is, wherever possible, scientific. Psychology proceeds in three stages. The first is observational, during which facts are recorded, analyzed and systematically classified. The second stage consists in devising hypotheses to explain the facts. In the third stage experiments are set up to test the hypotheses. These methods are not the prerogative of an expensively trained few. Anyone interested in doing so and who has the necessary time, energy and persistence, may become a sound and reliable psychologist in the sense mentioned above, and it is hoped that many of those who have courage enough to read further will be inspired to do so in due course.

By means of such systematic observations and experiments a good deal has been discovered about the mind, and in this book an attempt has been made to collect this material together and present it to those interested in horses. Unfortunately, for economic and practical reasons horses are not the most suitable of laboratory animals. It is true that in the days when naturalists were making their first observations on animal behaviour they were also as a rule travelling to their places of work in horse-drawn vehicles. In those days the horse was a most valued friend and assistant, and some interesting anecdotes were recorded of his behaviour. But side by side with progress in scientific techniques the horse has become ever more an expensive luxury. As a thing to be played with he cannot compete against guinea-pigs, rats, birds, dogs, cats, and monkeys. Hence a good deal of this book must consist of accounts of the behaviour of other animals. Yet despite the horror shown by one famous Irish horseman that 'one of God's favourite craichures should be likened to the rat' the principles discovered by laboratory experiments have a wide and general application and throw much light on horses as well. At the same time the horse is unique among animals in many respects, and one of the dangers scientists have learned to guard against in recent years is overgeneralisation.

It would be a mistake to give the impression that everything possible about the mind is already known. Its workings, especially in animals such as the horse, still retain many mysteries and there are countless problems still awaiting study. Wherever possible, I have tried to draw attention to these, suggesting ways in which they might be investigated further, to the benefit of man as well as horse.

Wherever possible, too, I have quoted from my own observations and described the behaviour of my own horses —not because I have any illusions that these are more interesting than other people's, but because it is always easier to understand and analyse a situation which has been observed first-hand rather than one which is described, however well, by others.

Despite these precautions, there will certainly be many who regard the facts quoted here as preposterous, absurd, or immaterial. Others will find nothing new. Psychology will remain to them, as it probably is now, merely another word

10

for commonsense. Between these two extremes I hope there may be some who will find added interest and enjoyment of horses as a result of learning something about the horse's mind, and who may by so doing make the lives of their mounts a little easier.

THE LOCATIONS

I said that wherever possible I have quoted my own observations. This being the case, and as most of the book centres around these descriptions, I must next introduce the places where most of these observations were carried out. The first, Stones Farm in Oxfordshire, was a thatched cottage surrounded by three-quarters of an acre of daffodils and fruit trees, majestically called 'The Park', together with a few primitive farm buildings and four small paddocks. There are many larger, many more elegant, and many more lavishly equipped places than Stones Farm, but few that would have suited me better. Stones Farm was so small and compact that on it one could see the horses the whole time. Even while they were out at grass and enjoying comparative freedom, they were still under observation from the house. While washing up in the kitchen or doing one's ablutions in the bathroom, it was possible to carry on a conversation with the horses in the stables or shout at others to get off the few square yards of 'garden' outside the front door. It was only necessary to walk a few paces from the sitting room to be in the centre of the 'estate' and be able to see at a glance what all the animals were doing. In this way it has been possible to see things and to make observations which in a larger and more luxurious place might well have passed unnoticed.

Because it was so small it was impossible to keep more than five or six horses at Stones Farm at one time. Although this limited the width and range of my experience, it had its compensations. With so small a population it was possible to get to know each individual thoroughly and to compare the behaviour of one with that of another under identical conditions.

After studying adult horses for a number of years, I began to realise that many of the idiosyncratic behaviour patterns

11

they exhibit might have an origin in earlier life. It was not enough to know all that a horse was experiencing here and now; it was necessary to know all that it had experienced throughout its life—and perhaps even what its parents had experienced before it was born. To do this meant breeding my own horses, but in order to breed healthy, useful horses, one must have space. In 1960 I therefore sold Stones Farm and moved to a larger, less compact holding near Buckingham. Leyland Farm, Gawcott, consisted of 100 acres of mainly permanent pasture; and for the first few years of my occupancy was run as a Dairy Farm on which one or two brood mares and their offspring ran with the cows.

As the years passed and the number of horses increased, the cows were gradually displaced, until by 1970 it was being run as a commercial Hunter Stud.

THE HORSES

Since the horses are the really important characters in this book, they deserve to be introduced next. It would clearly be impossible to introduce individually all the horses I have known who, voluntarily or involuntarily, have helped to mould the attitudes and opinions which are going to find expression here.

The first equine inhabitants of Stones Farm were named in numerical sequence; but in order to camouflage the bare numbers and to suggest a hint of classicism, rather free Latin translations were used wherever possible. This was all right from one (Unus) to ten (Decima), but after that the system began to break down. Undecim and Dodecim are not names that tripped lightly off the tongue, so that from then on the horses were named after Shakespearean characters. One of them, Portia, was a particularly important resident at Stones Farm who participated in one series of experiments I conducted on riding without a bit.

As well as the horses mentioned above, all of whom belonged to me personally for most of the time they were under observation, Stones Farm took in several paying guests and lodgers whose activities feature in some of the episodes to be described. They can be introduced briefly.

12

Peter was a 13-hand roan gelding of Irish origin, aged eleven, who belonged to one of my assistants.

Swanny was a three-year-old brown hunter mare who was turned out to grass at Stones Farm from the autumn of 1952 till the summer of 1953.

Nuts was a heavy-weight ten-year-old chestnut gelding of Irish origin who was at livery at Stones Farm during the 1953–54 season.

Fair Lady was a 15-hand, three-year-old chestnut Anglo-Arab mare who came to be broken and schooled in the spring of 1954.

Billy Bunter was a brown, four-year-old, Fell-type gelding who, although only with us for four months managed to find his way into nearly every one of the episodes described.

When I moved to Leyland Farm, I took with me a mare I had bought the previous year, Nuki, and her yearling daughter Nauri. Nuki and her descendents (which include one of her sons, Gamesman, and his offspring) gradually took over the whole of Leyland Farm, as already mentioned.

THE OBSERVERS

To name individually all the people whose observations and remarks have been mentioned here or who have been instrumental in deciding some attitude or experiment would be impossible.

At Stones Farm I was assisted by a series of girls usually fresh from school who slaved in the sun, paddled in the rain, were kicked by fighting horses and sworn at by an irate employer—who themselves took part in a number of experiments or carried out a variety of observations, at the same time as taking care of the much less exciting routine of running the establishment. Without their enthusiasm and interest, their care of the livestock, and their labour in the house, this book could not have been written.

At Leyland Farm the first necessity was to keep the place running and solvent while the various horse families grew up. I am eternally indebted to two couples, the Hunts and the Ashtons for their assistance in this matter.

Lastly I had better introduce myself. Almost my earliest

memories are of horses. They were my big passion in life, the centre of my childhood, and I was lucky enough to own a succession of ponies which, although by present day standards might not have been considered first-class, were good enough to provide me with a lot of fun and satisfaction. In common with many other girls before and since, my dearest ambition was to own a string of the finest animals in the country, to win prizes in all the big shows, and to lead the field continually when out hunting. But just as I was attaining an age when this might have become possible, and when my mother (despairing that I would ever become either an intellectual or a 'lady') bought me a really magnificent horse, with the contrariness typical of adolescence my interests changed.

I began to wonder what made living things breathe and move, what the stars were like, what part man played in the universe. Above all, I wanted to know about the mind—what it was, where it existed and how it worked—and in order to find out these things I had to go to a University and attend regular classes. Since then I have managed to earn enough money as a practicing Clinical Psychologist to keep a few horses. However, it has never been quite clear to myself, or others, whether I am primarily a psychologist who studies horses as a hobby, or vice versa.

CHAPTER 1

URGES AND INSTINCTS

The new grass had begun to grow at last. There was a cold wind blowing, but when the sun shone between showers it had an enlivening warmth. The day had come to turn the hunters out—not only for a few hours each day in the park, as we had been doing for the last few weeks, but for good—for a long rest. Nuts and Unus showed their approval by thrusting their heads straight down into the grass the moment their head-collars were removed, and turning their backs on us. The ponies at the far end of the field pricked their ears and within a few seconds came galloping over to greet the new arrivals. There were a few scuffles, a few sniffs, a squeal or two, and a flurry of heels, and then all galloped away together in a bunch. They had settled down, we thought, and we began to wander off. But when we looked back, something else was happening. Septem, the little black gelding and Nuts, the big chestnut hunter, were standing on their hind legs, pawing at each other like two contestants in a boxing-match. They dropped down again, and Septem laid back his ears and made a grab at Nuts' withers. The big horse arched his neck, recoiled a step, and then lunged forward to attack in his turn. Septem wheeled round, cantered off a couple of strides, and then turned on his hind legs again. Nuts followed suit, and once more the pawing and boxing started. The match went on for several minutes; then one of the contestants broke off, apparently bored, and went in search of food.

This was not the only match which took place at that time

or which we had a chance to see. Later on that day, and frequently during the succeeding weeks, exhibitions of the sort could be witnessed in the fields around Stones Farm at almost any time. Sometimes four of the five geldings would be performing such antics together, rearing and prancing in pairs like dancers in a quadrille. There seemed to be no point in it, and no animosity. The game would start slowly and almost as if by chance. One horse would walk up to another and take a friendly sniff at its withers. He in turn would shake his head, lash his tail, and turn round, stamping with one fore-foot. The game would then start and would continue with mock biting and mock kicking until one of them refused to play further. What were they doing? What was the object of it all?

It is possible, of course, just to note this sort of behaviour, describe it, call it 'instinctive', and pass on. But to give a thing a name is not to understand or explain it. Besides, what do we mean by 'instinctive'?

An instinct used to be considered as a rigid and inflexible chain of reactions, designed to serve some internal biological need but which was triggered off by a stimulus from the environment. Instinctive acts were thought to be carried out in the same pattern by all members of a species, although individuals might have no previous experience to guide them nor any idea of the ends to be achieved.

But if this is what is meant by an instinct, then the mock battles which I have just described cannot have been instinctive. It is true that the general pattern of behaviour was the same among all the horses, but each individual treated it in his own way. Septem was gay and light. His favourite sally was a quick dart at the withers or quarters of his opponent, followed by an equally agile retreat. Nuts, on the other hand, was cumbersome and slow. He approached his adversary like a heavy tank, flaying his front legs ahead of him and pounding on, come what might. Unus, the bay, and Octavius, a grey cob, were rather self-conscious and coy about their games: they would only dance when they thought no one was looking, and even then they wore expressions suggesting that they were doing it merely to

16

please others. None of these actions was rigid, nor were any of them designed to serve any obvious biological need. The end, as I have said, was usually flat and indecisive. No obvious dominance was claimed; no mating followed.

The observation of other animals has shown that the old conception of instincts applies to these little better than it does to the spring-time battles of my horses. In the first place, very few animals carry out their instinctive acts exactly in the same way each time. The patterns of behaviour are not rigid. In the second place, almost all animals—even insects— can modify their inborn reactions if the need arises, and they frequently do so, profiting by past experience. Inborn instinctive acts are not, therefore, necessarily inflexible. In the third place, many apparently instinctive reactions are in reality handed down by tradition rather than inheritance. A good example of this can be found in jackdaws as described by Konrad Lorenz.[26] When jackdaws are first hatched, they have no instinctive knowledge of their natural enemies. A young bird reared in isolation will allow a preying dog or cat to creep up on it without showing the least suspicion of impending danger. Very soon, however, it will learn to suspect all those creatures which the members of its community indicate are to be feared. Is this instinct or is it intelligence?

Yet another objection to the old definition of instincts comes from considering the times at which instinctive activity is shown. Instinctive acts are not performed indiscriminately on all occasions: they are only evident when an internal need is active and calls for them.[35] Birds, although they are born with the knowledge of the sort of material to collect for a nest of their particular species, only collect material at all when it is nest-building time.

What, then, is one to call these acts? Shall we redefine the word 'instinct' so as to cover all these points, or shall we leave it out and use entirely different terms? The easiest thing seems to be to drop the word 'instinct' and to describe animal behaviour in other ways. Once a word has had a certain meaning attached to it, it is difficult to divorce it from that meaning; and by continuing to use the word itself

17

misunderstandings may arise. For this reason it has been found more helpful and convenient nowadays to consider animal behaviour under three headings:

(1) the urges, drives, needs and motives inspiring it;
(2) the stimuli necessary to set it off; and
(3) the patterns of behaviour which result.

This chapter will deal only with the urges, needs, drives and motives of action. The stimuli arousing behaviour and the behaviour itself will be considered more fully later on.

It must be pointed out, however, that these divisions are purely arbitrary and are made solely for convenience. There is much overlapping and much inter-action between them. A weak drive and a strong stimulus, for instance, may produce just the same result as a strong drive and a weak stimulus.

The needs of horses are many and various, but for the sake of clarity and simplicity it is helpful to group certain ones together and to consider them as a class.

NEED FOR FOOD AND WATER

These needs are so fundamental, it might be thought that very little could be said about them. However, this does not really follow. The more fundamental a need, the more closely it must be involved in all aspects of living, and hence the more carefully it should be considered.

Among humans so many activities are associated symbolically with food, and so many rites and customs are accompanied by eating, that their description and discussion have filled many books. Some primitive people believe that by eating the things they idolize they will become more like them, and that a promise made over food and drink is more binding than one made in other conditions. These ideas have become incorporated into many religious practices and social customs, and can be seen even in our own societies. It is only necessary to consider our City dinners and wedding banquets to realize that this is so.

Although the taking of food has not become so involved in social customs in all other forms of the animal world as it has in man, it nevertheless occupies a large part of their daily lives. Moreover, the way in which an individual animal takes

18

its food often epitomizes its whole character. Some horses will eat whatever is put before them quietly and without fuss, will finish up what they are given and go away grateful. But these are in the minority. Unus, a highly strung thoroughbred who never carried much weight, would get into a dither of anticipation as soon as he saw his bucket being prepared. He whinnied every time his box was approached, as if he had never been fed before. But no sooner was the bucket finally put in front of him than he thrust his nose to its bottom and scooped the contents on to the floor. If the corn was carefully picked up and replaced, it was thrown out again; but if it was left where he had thrown it he would quietly go over the floor after one had departed, picking up every grain.

If a piece of carrot or a handful of corn was offered to Septem or to Octavius, they would take it quietly and lick over the palm of one's hand afterwards. Quinque and Billy Bunter, two native ponies, on the other hand, would snatch at it as if half starved and then try to scrape one's palm with their teeth.

But although individual differences in the way a need is satisfied may be seen in different horses, the need for food and water affects the daily lives of all animals in certain uniform and very fundamental ways. As a higher percentage of the body is composed of water than of solids, so an animal's need for drink is greater than its need for food. This has been demonstrated by experiments on rats.[7] A rat in a state of need was put at one end of a tunnel, with bait—in the form of what he needed—at the other end. To get the bait the rat had to pass over a grid which could be electrified with any strength of current the experimenter liked to use. The stronger the current, the more unpleasant it was for the rat to pass over. The experimenter gradually increased the current in the grid until the rat refused to pass over it. He found that rats would pass over far greater currents (i.e., would face considerably greater pain) in order to get to water than to get to food.

When looking for food and drink however, animals are not indiscriminate. The body is so made that an appetite is usually developed for the particular type of nourishment needed. An animal deprived of salt will seek salty foods; one short of fat will prefer fatty foods.

The extent to which horses are able to pick out food elements which they particularly need has not been demonstrated scientifically, but anyone who has allowed a horse to walk along a roadside with its head down eating whatever it wants to is usually surprised by the variety and type of plant they choose, and by the very definite way in which a horse will pick out one and reject others. One lady kept a careful list of her pony's choices throughout the seasons noting that some plants were taken in the Spring but rejected in the Autumn. This has been confirmed by a series of experiments carried out at the Equine Research Station in Newmarket.[2]

As a rule, grass near places where dung or urine has been dropped are not grazed readily,[31] but new-born foals may nibble and ingest small quantities of their dam's dung.[34] It is thought that this may be because the dung of a nursing mare contains beneficial elements to a young foal.

There is a tendency for all wild animals to avoid eating the plants likely to harm them, but the number of cases of poisoning by ragwort, ivy and other weeds often recorded, indicate that nature is not infallible. Some people believe that horses (as well perhaps as many other species) learn by example what plants can or cannot be eaten. They point out that despite the presence of many Yew trees in the New Forest,[42] cases of Yew poisoning are almost non-existent among the animals raised there. It is also widely recognised that some items which horses will become passionately fond of once they have acquired the taste for them (e.g. sugar, peppermints, apples, carrots) are not taken to quickly, while others which are recommended for veterinary reasons (worm-dose, cod liver oil, bonemeal) are only accepted reluctantly if at all.

Sometimes appetites may be psychologically inspired. Professor Masserman[28] was once investigating artificially induced neuroses in cats (*see* Chapter VI) and found in the course of his observations that 'neurotic' cats often preferred milk laced with alcohol to plain milk, although normal cats and those which had recovered from their neuroses appeared to abhor liquor.

20

The amount, as well as the type, of nourishment an animal takes depends on its mental as well as on its physical state. Fear, apprehension, agitation and excitement are notoriously detrimental to the appetite, and animals in these conditions do not seem to feel the need for food as much as others. This is because the body is so organized that mental stress activates small glands within it which liberate into the blood-stream reserve supplies of energy from emergency food stores in the fat and liver. Biologically, of course, this mechanism serves a useful purpose. An excited or agitated animal is usually one involved in fighting, fleeing or mating— some condition in which it may have to travel long distances at great speed. On such occasions the less time the animal takes off for food, the better. However, the gain can only be temporary, and the mechanism must be reserved for emergencies. If the animal is too often in a state of agitation or apprehension, the body quickly eats into its reserves of food and begins to lose condition. This is only too frequently the case with horses which work themselves into frenzies during the hunting season and refuse to eat when returned to their stables at night.

The phenomenon of 'going off' food because of some other need or urge is perhaps easier to understand than its opposite—eating used to satisfy needs other than hunger. Yet the latter also occurs. A man who eats at a dinner party does not necessarily do so because he is hungry. He may be eating because he is prompted by the desire to appear sociable and not to embarrass his host, or because he is bored by the company of those sitting beside him. Similarly, animals that are in need of things other than food may often try to satisfy their cravings in a distorted way by eating abnormal quantities. Feeding may even become a sort of nervous twitch which an animal employs to calm itself, in the same way that humans smoke. When Unus was out hunting he was in a perpetual quiver of excitement and continually snatched at little mouthfuls of grass or anything else available. As soon as the mad rush started he would be off in the forefront, leaves, sticks and tufts protruding from the corners of his mouth. At the first sign of a pause down would go his head again. Sometimes I feel that the habit was merely a ruse employed to get his head free and the reins long so that he would not be impeded from going off as soon as the moment came. Whatever the reason, however, this wild snatching at food was almost exclusively associated with excitement.

The extent and voracity of an animal's appetite depends not only on its hunger but also on the way in which the food is presented—i.e., not only on the need but also on the stimulus. Human beings are well aware of this fact in themselves. If food is served up badly, the appetite can be ruined. If choicely presented, however, a person may be tempted to eat long after he ceases to be hungry.

The same rule applies to animals, although the things which stimulate their appetites are often on a rather different level to those which stimulate the appetite of humans. Normally if a chicken is thrown a handful of corn it will only go on eating until it has satisfied its immediate hunger. But if, after it has stopped picking at the grains on the ground, a few more grains are thrown down, it will start eating again. If it stops and more grains are thrown down, it will have another spell of eating. This sequence of events may be continued for some time. Moreover, even if a chicken has already eaten its normal fill, it can be induced to start again by the sight of another feeding. In other words, the eating reaction can be set off in chickens not only by the sight of food but even more readily by the sight of moving food and by the sight of others feeding.

These principles apply to horses no less than to chickens, although in the case of the former it is difficult to lay down hard and fast rules. Some horses eat better when they are alone than in company; others do the very reverse and eat better when in company. Some like their meals 'little and often'; others are difficult to interest in food, but, once started, will clear up what is in front of them.

By paying attention to the psychological as well as to the physiological factors associated with feeding, those horses which are 'bad-doers' can often be persuaded to take what they might otherwise leave.

Although all horse owners will agree on certain basic

dietary needs in their charges, there is probably as much variation of opinion about the best way of feeding horses as there is about bringing up children. There is no doubt that certain people have a knack of keeping their animals well and fit and sleek, while others do not; but what a good feeder does, he is very often unable to say himself. Like a good cook he tends to break the rules rather than go by the recipes.

The fact that diet needs to be altered with the amount of work a horse is doing is usually recognized, but why alterations of diet alter what might be regarded as temperament as well as fitness, has seldom been considered. All riders know that a horse full of oats becomes 'fresh'—that is to say it is liable to buck, plunge, pull, shy, jiggle and dance—but why? It seems to be generally accepted that this is just a horse's way of 'letting off steam' but as I shall be discussing later on, I feel it may also have the effect, intentional or not, of raising an individual's position in the 'dominance' hierarchy. These antics could well be a form of threat, by means of which the animal is testing-out its own position in the social order.

There is yet another aspect of eating, the understanding of which is valuable to riders and especially to those concerned with the breaking and schooling of horses. It is usually maintained that the way to an animal's heart is through it's stomach, and that the only way to show an animal that it has done well is by giving it something to eat as a reward. With those animals which eat spasmodically, like dogs, this is probably the case; but horses are among the group of animals which take in food for long periods of the day. A little bit extra now and then cannot seem very important to them. Moreover, they must be so accustomed to various incidents occurring during the course of a grazing session that a course of lungeing or a jump or two between mouthfuls can have little more significance to them than the flight of a bird or the mooing of a cow. This is not to say that they do not learn to associate certain people with tit-bits; that they do not get used to being fed at certain signs; or that they do not anticipate food rewards with considerable pleasure. All it does suggest is that they may not necessarily associate the

23

reward with the things that they did to deserve it in the same way as a man would do. When I first schooled Unus to jump, I always kept my pockets full of oats, and after he had done well I would lean forward with some grains in my hand. After some days of this, he came to associate my leaning forward with rewards. No sooner did I move in the saddle than he would stop and swing his head round in anticipation. However, he never showed the same interest and expectation before I moved, no matter how well he had jumped. In other words, he appeared to associate the presence of a reward not with his own performance but only with the movement which immediately preceded it.

Although the giving of food rewards has become a firm practice in 'training by kindness', it is not an essential part of it. This was proved by the case of Quinque. Quinque was a half-bred New Forest pony whom I bought as a three-year-old straight from the wild Thames-side scrubland where she was bred. She had never been touched by man before, nor had she eaten anything but marsh reeds and a little straw. Like many of those with which she was raised, she had had the misfortune to be caught by the East Coast floods of February, 1953, and she was a most pathetic little sight as we drove her into my trailer when I went to collect her. Her coat was caked with mud and salt and was falling out in handfuls. Her back was almost bare and was coverd with sore patches. She was shivering with fright and loneliness and only pecked occasionally at mouthfuls of straw from the floor of the trailer.

On arrival she was put into a large box and immediately started to eat her bed of clean straw with relish, totally ignoring the pile of sweet hay which had also been provided. By evening she had calmed down to the extent that I was able to put my hand on her shoulder and gently rub at a little of the caked mud. This seemed to put her into ecstasies. She stood with an expression of bliss on her face, and as soon as I stopped my share of the activity she continued to rub herself up against me as against a post. Before nightfall she was racing up to the door of her box every time she saw one of us approach it and was offering her head, back or neck for massage. Our food offerings, meanwhile, failed to arouse the slightest response. Buckets of corn, handfuls of sugar, apples and carrots, all were sniffed disdainfully and pushed aside. She would have nothing to eat but straw.

Quinque's training started the next day, and she was the easiest and quietest animal to handle that I have ever known, as well as being one of the quickest to learn. But she never accepted a single reward of food, however frequently and in whatever variety these were offered. When we wanted to tell her that she had done well, we would rub the side of her neck or the salty patches on her back, and this seemed to give her all the recompense she needed. After several months Quinque became more sophisticated in her tastes and, probably learning from the example of others, found various delicacies quite palatable. By that time, however, the attempt to give her food rewards had been abandoned, and she continued to respond contentedly to a little scratch on her neck long after the irritation of the flood water had passed off.

Although food may have little meaning as an occasional reward of the usual type, it has a useful part to play in other spheres of training. Horses very soon come to associate those who handle them with tit-bits, and once this association has been established they show much less fear than before when asked by the same person to do strange and unnatural things.

There are some trainers, admittedly, who do not approve of this, and who consider 'discipline' better than bribery, but it is possible by providing palatable food, to make a horse submit to, and even enjoy, experiences it might otherwise resent.

I was once breaking in a wild and obstreperous three-year-old gelding who was not only suspicious of man but very possessive of his equine companions. To begin with he did not appear to resent our daily breaking sessions too much, but by degrees they seemed to become increasingly irksome to him. By the end of a week he showed signs of becoming a real problem. At the sight of the breaking tackle, his ears would go back and he would prepare to kick.

As soon as I noticed these inauspicious signs I took to filling my pockets with oats; at intervals throughout our sessions, he would be offered a few from my hand. Although he seldom ate more than the odd grain, their very presence was enough to reassure him. Soon he was greeting the appearance of the tackle with pleasure rather than dislike and preparing to chase away any of his companions who tried to usurp my attention.

Moreover, food can be given in order to take a horse's mind off what might otherwise be considered as an unpleasant experience, such as shoeing, clipping, etc. When Septem first came to us as an unbroken two-year-old, it was impossible to get a hand near his legs or pick up his feet. Any attempt to touch him below the shoulder would arouse all the resistance of which his strong body was capable. Because of this, one of the first things he naturally did was to get himself entangled in a wire fence; and we found him one day trotting round the field with open leg wounds which obviously needed dressing. The treating of these was extremely hazardous and was not accomplished without some casualties. This made me decide that we must do something about him before the situation was repeated. One of my assistants and I spent many weeks coaxing and fondling him and moving our hands slowly up and down his legs. As soon as we got anywhere near the cannon-bone, however, he would be up in the air and thrashing out violently. In the end we decided that, badly as he was behaving and little as he deserved it, we would try distracting him with a bucket of corn while the handling was being carried out. This was immediately successful. A few irritated stamps were all he had time for between mouthfuls, and before he knew it his feet were being lifted and picked out. Once the habit had been established and he found that no harm came to him, the corn was reduced and finally removed altogether.

Instances in which feeding is involved in learning and in the assessment of other forms of animal behaviour will constantly be mentioned in the following pages, and will not therefore be dealt with further here.

SELF-PROTECTION

There are two principal methods of self-protection known

to animals: flight and fight. The majority of horses seem to prefer the former, only resorting to the latter when cornered, and in their wild state they must spend a considerable amount of time fleeing from enemies, real or suspected. At the present time, however, when horses are protected from most of their natural enemies, it might appear unnecessary to say very much more on this subject; yet the fact that the drive to escape basically exists in horses can often explain a number of their otherwise incomprehensible acts. Any situation in which a horse feels itself to be unsafe may fire off self-protective behaviour, from which it follows that if a horse starts showing behaviour of a self-protective nature it may be suffering from a sense of insecurity.

One of the most obvious instances of flight in horses is a reluctance to being caught in the field. If a horse is difficult to catch, therefore, it must feel that some trouble is in store for it. This is obvious, but what is very often not so obvious is the aspect of its treatment that the horse is frightened of. Not all horses are frightened of the same things, and the difficulty of discovering the cause of fear in an individual case can be illustrated by the story of Septem.

As far as I know, Septem's only contact with humans before I bought him as a two-year-old was to be gelded two months previously—not, perhaps, an experience most likely to endear him to the human race! On arriving at Stones Farm he showed intense suspicion of all our advances, although after several days of petting, stroking and hand feeding he softened so far as to come towards us when we approached him, both while he was in the stable and at the end of a long tether. When this state had been reached I judged that the time had come when he might be turned out with the others. Although for the first few days of liberty he made no move towards us if we went near him, he did not actively attempt to run away either, and by the end of a week's hand feeding and petting he was walking up to us as freely and readily as his companions.

Having got this far, I decided we might start a little serious training and began him in a head-collar. He seemed to regard this as a game, and his friendliness in the field increased.

27

Training progressed so fast that within a fortnight I had a saddle on him. At the beginning of each new move, and before he would submit to any new piece of saddlery being placed on him, he showed intense suspicion, but his fear usually seemed to be overcome within the first few minutes of the novelty. After he had been lunged in a saddle for three days, I decided he was ready to be mounted. He submitted to the mounting process without any great show of horror, but when he was asked to move forward the heavens broke and we had a nasty scene. After carrying me several times round the field at great speed, he finally agreed to walk forward a few yards at a more dignified pace; but he was obviously very much averse to the whole procedure and unmollified even when I finally dismounted. The next day Septem was very difficult to catch, and even proffered tit-bits failed to tempt him within reach. By luring him into a stable after other horses, he was caught and mounted on several further occasions, and was ridden daily for about a week. However, his fear of the saddle seemed to be increasing rather than decreasing, and at the same time he was becoming ever more difficult to approach in the field.

There were several factors which could have accounted for Septem's difficulty over being caught at this time. In the first place, one of the mares was in season, and, having been gelded so short a time, Septem was very interested in her. In the second place, I was in the process of changing assistants, and Septem may have been suspicious of the newcomers. In the third place, there might have been a dislike of the saddle; in the fourth place, I might have gone altogether too fast and have asked him to learn more than his young mind was capable of absorbing. As I was unable to make up my mind with which of these causes the difficulty lay, I decided to abandon the fight and leave Septem to recover his confidence in his own time.

It was about two months before he again approached a human voluntarily, but when he found that the bucket being carried was full of oats and that he was once again allowed to eat it unmolested his courage increased rapidly, and it was not long before he was once again being caught and led about without trouble. During the next two weeks we gradually went through the handling and breaking process in the same way as before. Septem's suspicions were only slightly less evident this time than on the previous occasion, and every new movement still appeared to arouse anxiety until it had been repeated several times over and accompanied by copious supplies of chopped apples. The first day I mounted him again, however, he seemed especially calm and docile. Nor did he show very much resistance to being sat upon. I did no more this time than remain on his back for a few seconds before dismounting—but the following day he was extremely difficult to catch. He seemed for all the world to have returned to the condition he was in after he had been mounted several months before, although this time there was no question of mares, changing assistants, or of having gone too fast. It was apparently only the saddle to which he objected. By persevering, we finally caught Septem and mounted him once more, and again he submitted to the procedure with apparent indifference. The following day, however, we failed to make contact with him at all except after he had been cornered and trapped. He spurned chopped apples—his favourite delicacy at this time—and stood when patted with his ears firmly back and his feet stubbornly together.

On this occasion I felt that I had better continue backing him, come what might, and resorted to the practice of feeding him continuously while he was being mounted. After three days of this routine, he seemed to recover his composure. He would stand like a rock of his own free will to be mounted and dismounted, and, thank goodness, he was never again the slightest difficulty to catch.

Refusing to be caught is a method of self-protection which can only be indulged in by horses at comparative liberty, such as those out at grass. Hence, when horses in the stable or under the saddle want to protect themselves they have to do so by fighting—that is to say, by kicking, rearing and bucking. The origin of these difficulties must again be looked for in the history of each individual case; in the history of the animal, the circumstances connected with the fight, and, just

29

as importantly, in the times when the animal seems to be at peace. But sometimes, after every possible cause has been explored and every possible reason discounted, an animal will still fight in his box or rear and kick when ridden. Is it possible to find a logical reason for the activities in these situations?

I believe it is, but the reason is not very readily apparent, and to understand it one must go back a long way. It is connected with the well-known fact that if a biologically useful reaction is not expressed for a long time the tendency to employ it gradually increases until finally it may be triggered off by any stimulus which provides an adequate excuse. Dogs which are thwarted of an opportunity to hunt will pick up a rag or stick and start worrying that. Over-anxious people who keep healthy during times of stress because they have every opportunity to exploit their anxiety openly find during peace that their inability to vent anxious behaviour leads to serious nervous breakdown. In just the same way, animals or birds which would naturally spend much of their time in flight from enemies tend, if not hunted, to fly from anything which approaches them. Thus, flocks of duck which have been left in peace for a long time will suddenly rise up in alarm on a calm evening, making off as they would do at the approach of a predator, even when there is not a moving object in sight. It is as if they are trying to keep in practice—carrying out peace-time manoeuvres.

Something of the same sort seems to occur in over-protected animals at the Zoo. It is not so much the desire to hunt and exercise themselves which, according to Dr Hediger,[15] Curator of the Basle Zoo, makes a wild animal pace its cage, but the pent-up and accumulated urge to escape from an absent enemy. After a severe fright, such as they may get if a gun is let off nearby or part of their cage falls in, their pacing frequently slows down or even stops altogether for a time.

Coming back again now to horses, there seems to be every likelihood that these animals too, if keyed up to activity and unable to give vent to their energies—in other words, when over-fresh—may shy, kick, bite and stamp, not because they are afraid, but, on the contrary, because they are short of a good fright and of an opportunity to let off steam. Quattuor, a grey hunter mare, was normally a most docile and placid creature, extremely hard to frighten and almost impossible to anger. However, about the middle of one season she hurt her knee and had to be kept in the stable on only a few minutes' walking exercise each day. After about a week of this unaccustomed rest she began to get very fidgety when being groomed and suddenly took to panicking at the sight of her own rug. For some days we tried to calm and soothe her as the rug was put on, placing it on her very gently and stroking her at the same time. This only seemed to make her worse. Then one evening I resorted to the opposite extreme and flapped it violently in front of her for the best part of an hour. She entered into this game with zest, leaping about, hitting her head on the roof and sides of her box, snorting, and pawing the ground. Finally she calmed down and allowed the rug to be thrown over her without further resistance. The following day she hardly flinched at the sight of the rug—but she suddenly began shying at her reflection in the window. We covered up the window so that there was no reflection. The next day she began shying at her shadow on the wall. This time she won. I could find no way of lighting the box without also causing a shadow, and Quattuor went on fleeing from her own shadow till her knee healed and she could get out hunting again. As soon as she was able to do this, her behaviour in the box once more became exemplary. However, towards the end of the next summer she was laid up once more. After several days of inactivity her shadow-shying reappeared and only stopped when she was again back in full work. Her behaviour was obviously not due to real fright, but to the accumulation of a fright-reaction which finally reached such a stage that it could be set off by almost anything.

It is possible that these situations may sometimes lead to far more serious consequences than was the case with Quattuor. Tertia, a three-year-old TB mare, though as docile as a lamb if continually entertained, was packed with aggression (generous people call it character). She enjoyed nothing so much as a good battle and, if bored, would pick a fight with anyone who happened to be handy. The one thing she did seem to have been successfully broken to when she first came to us was traffic, and she would pass any kind of vehicle, from milk lorries to racing motor-cycles, without turning a hair. During the early part of her first hunting season, when she was beginning to shape well and the basic part of her schooling seemed to be firmly laid, there was a long spell of cold weather which stopped hunting and made exercising difficult. Dreary walks along the roadside were all that could be undertaken. Then, to add to the already considerable peril of exercising, Tertia began shying at traffic. At first only the largest and heaviest vehicles upset her, but within the space of a few days she was behaving like a terrified two-year-old in the presence of anything that moved at all. As in the case of Quattuor with the rug, attempts to calm and reassure her seemed only to make matters worse. Since I had a suspicion that her behaviour was mainly due to boredom, I was hesitant to resort to the obvious alternative of punishing her, especially as I was afraid of thereby establishing in her an ingrained association between traffic and discomfort which might result in her really being afraid of traffic in the future. I decided therefore that if she wanted to have a good fight she should have it—only not on the road. Despite the 18 ins. of snow in the field, she was exercised there the next day, and went through every manoeuvre it was possible to do. She skidded, stumbled, tripped and slipped, but appeared to enjoy it immensely and frequently got her own back by suddenly lying down when her rider was least expecting it, and having a good roll. When she went back on to the roads again after the thaw, she gave a slight quiver at the first lorry she saw and was never any further trouble.

Fear, and a sense of insecurity in general, often lead horses to attack others with unprovoked ferocity, and cause them to behave in a way which might easily be misinterpreted. Billy Bunter, a four-year-old Fell pony who had been broken when I got him, is an example of such a case. Although extremely domineering and bossy among the herd, he was unaccountably nervous of everything connected with being ridden. He

32

was terrified of traffic, and always tried to get back to other horses or to his stable. The world, in fact, was to him a very dangerous place. During the first weeks he was with us many of his rides were difficult. He was made to do things he had obviously never done before and to go places which he considered it was most unwise for a horse to venture. When returned to the field after such a difficult ride, he would lay back his ears and go for poor Unus with frightening violence, attacking the old horse again and again without either provocation or reason. If on the other hand his ride had been straightforward and easy and there had not been any trouble, he would pay no attention to either Unus or any other horse when put back into the field, but would begin grazing peacefully right away.

Nona showed the same association in reverse. Henpecked and bullied by her equine companions in the field, she would, after a particularly trying afternoon, take it out on the first human being who came within reach. It was possible to tell just how much she had been chivvied and bitten by her companions during the day by her attitude towards us in the evenings.

Fleeing and fighting, however, like eating—and, for that matter, any other activity—may be used to satisfy needs other than those which normally arouse them. Animals that are deprived of food, of company, or of sexual gratification, often become restive and pugnacious, and an example of what may result was demonstrated by Swanny.

This three-year-old brown mare was very highly sexed and found little satisfaction in the poor geldings with whom she had to spend her time at Stones Farm. Whenever she came into season, and if not fully occupied by being rigorously schooled, she would corner one after another of the horses in the field, kicking and biting each in turn until it was a mass of cuts.

Swanny demonstrated self-protective activity used to satisfy other needs; but self-protective needs can also be satisfied by reactions inappropriate to them. One spring, when Unus had a bad leg and had been turned out in the field off work for some weeks, with the need for a good fight

33

steadily increasing, I was told that he had been seen playing with sticks like a dog. He would pick up a stick in his mouth, so the story went, toss it over his head, and then canter after it, bucking. I thought this story very far-fetched and was inclined to disbelieve it. However, the following day Unus was standing by the gate with the other horses when I went to see them, and as I approached to talk to him I noticed that he had a short, thick stick in his mouth. I put out my hand to take it, but just at the last moment he snatched his head away, turned on his quarters, and went bucking off across the field, tossing his head to and fro until finally he let go of the stick and sent it sailing over his back. He stopped, turned sharply, and retraced his steps as if to look for it, but by that time the game seemed to have palled, and after a very cursory and unsuccessful search he came back to the gate.

SEX AND REPRODUCTION

Although the reproductive urge has often been considered one of the most fundamental and, from the point of view of survival of the species, is probably the most vital, very little is mentioned about this subject in most of the books on horses. But in view of what is known in other species it seems more than probable that the sexual need colours many aspects of a horse's general behaviour.

The strength of the sexual need is closely associated with the physiological state of an animal, and this, as is well known, varies in most species at different seasons of the year. Closely corresponding to the distribution and frequency of the sexual cycle is the degree to which animals incorporate sexual activity in their general behaviour. Those species which can mate all the year round, such as monkeys and apes, employ sexual behaviour for a number of different purposes, such as to trap enemies, to gain allies, and to assert leadership. According to Professor Zuckerman[51] a baboon will use the almost irresistible stimulus of 'presenting' itself in order to lure a rival within reach. As soon as the hated adversary puts out a hand to touch it, the cunning tempter will turn and bite its fingers. A female baboon will also make advances to one that is tormenting her so that her jealous

34

overlord shall come to her assistance and chastise the tormentor. A low-caste female who dares to take food before her overlord has finished eating will immediately present herself to him so that he will be more occupied with courting her than with snatching away the food.

Animals with short and seasonal reproductive seasons, on the other hand, tend to have much more selective and clearly defined sexual behaviour, which is only seen at times of mating. In such animals the act of mating itself cannot occur unless it is preceded by a series of preliminary steps, each of which is dependent on selected events from the phase before it.

It is usually assumed, and often preached, that sexual activity in animals is far more natural and healthy than it is in man; but from the few instances which have just been quoted it will be clear that this is not necessarily the case. Some of the 'perversion' and 'aberrations' seen in animals would in fact put many of the Sunday newspapers in the shade. Even parenthood is not without its dangers. Nursing mothers will not only adopt and suckle the young of others if these are put with their own off-spring, but barren females will even steal the young of different species, producing milk to feed them, and guarding them from their rightful relatives. One reason for these phenomena lies in the fact that, as has already just been explained, each part of the reproductive process is an act in itself and is a purely automatic response to particular stimuli from the outside world. If an object provides the appropriate cue, the animal will and must respond to it, blindly and immediately. If the cue is lacking, whatever the other characteristics of the object, the effect will be nil. For instance, to male frogs in season the signal to mate is 'movement in an object of a certain size'. Anything of the required size that moves is a sufficient stimulus to arouse mating responses in the male, whether it be a piece of stick or a moving weed. If, on the other hand, a female frog floats up motionless among a swarm of males, she is left unmolested.

At the same time, however, it must never be forgotten that the sensitivity of an animal to the 'sign' or releasing stimulus depends on the strength of the inner urge or need. If the need has been allowed to accumulate, the response will always be liberated by a weaker stimulus than that normally required; but an animal that has recently satisfied a need will only react to the presence of a strong and appropriate stimulus. Hence, an animal that has all the sexual satisfaction it needs will not respond to a sign that does not fill the bill in all possible respects; whereas one that has been cooped up and unsatisfied for a long time will respond to the first likely object that comes its way. Baboons will normally show very little sexual interest in an animal of another species, but a baboon that has been kept in solitude for long may make advances to dogs and any other animals of a suitable size. Again, a nursing mother will seldom go out of her way to adopt the young of others, although she may accept them if they are put with her own. But a barren female in whom the maternal urge is strong and pent-up through lack of satisfaction may face great hardships and pain to find some object on which to lavish her affections. Thus, most of the aberrations seen among animals are due to abnormal conditions and can therefore quite rightly be regarded as abnormal in themselves.

Yet very often the cause of such an abnormality is difficult to find. It may lie in some obvious and readily righted shortage, such as in the cases mentioned above, or it may be due to dissatisfaction in another sphere—i.e., to the presence of another need whose existence is temporarily masked. In some cases, however, the origin of the aberration may lie even deeper, in disturbances which must now be discussed.

It has been mentioned, and is quite self-evident, that the reproductive urge is largely dependent on physical development. An immature animal which cannot mate shows little interest in the objects and stimuli associated with this activity. But sex is not the only activity which parallels physical development. At every stage of its growth the body and mind develop specific needs and requirements which, if not satisfied at that time, seem to leave a permanent defect in the adult later on. Rats during their normal development go through a phase of hoarding food. If they are prevented from hoarding at the time when this need is most active, they will start hoarding every time they are hungry during later life. It is as if the need which was not gratified at the normal time can never fully be satisfied later on. The animal is for ever trying to catch up on what has been lost. In much the same way, according to some investigators, small children who are deprived of parental affection during their early years show a permanent lack of stability and self-confidence later on which becomes evident whenever they are up against any difficult situation. This principle is basic to all needs and is only mentioned in this section because deprivation of one need or another during maturation so often seems to affect adult sexual behaviour.

In Great Britain the majority of horses put to work are either females or castrated (gelded) males, but in many other countries the riding of females is regarded as highly dangerous. There it is only the males—entire or castrated—which are used. In either case, the segregation of the sexes is regarded as of prime importance unless or until breeding is desired. Even where procreation is intended, this is seldom left entirely to nature. One, and only one, stallion is customarily turned out with a group of mares; but the traditional picture of the stallion as a dominant Lord, leading a group of mares out of danger, finding them shelter and protecting them from enemies, finds little confirmation in real life. In fact even among wild zebras it is usually a boss female which leads the herd, the stallion following along behind, either at the rear of the bunch or to one side of it.[22],[37]

The same tendency has been recorded by S. J. Tyler in New Forest ponies. Most mornings and evenings, groups of these ponies make 'treks' of up to one mile to seek water, food or shade. The start of the trek might be instigated by any of the group members, but once on the move, each family group will be headed by the dam, whose offspring follow her in single file, while the stallion brings up the rear. Nor is the stallion necessarily boss in his own home. One summer my own stallion, Gamesman, was turned out with a neighbour's mare (I will call her A) when, after they had been together for some weeks, another mare B was put in with them. Mare A, who had been violently possessive of

Gamesman up till then, but had herself been satisfied by him, was determined not to allow the newcomer to alienate his affections. But now a curious circle came to be evolved. Instead of driving the new mare away from the stallion, mare A drove the stallion away from the new mare and took possession of B herself. Poor Gamesman was left standing alone while the two mares flicked the flies off one another's noses and monopolised all the choicest shade. Even when mare B 'came into use' the second time, Gamesman was not allowed near enough to cover her. The two mares, fighting and kicking, galloped around the paddock keeping him at bay. It was not till A had been removed from the field that B turned to the stallion, but the moment he had given her what she momentarily desired she was racing away again around the hedges calling for her former female companion.[46]

SOCIALIZATION AND COMPANY

That horses are gregarious by nature and tend to wander about in herds, is a fact which needs little emphasis. But that the need for company is often so strong and deep that it may affect an individual's whole personality and behaviour, is one which is often overlooked. We get so used to seeing horses ridden about singly or turned out in fields alone, that it is easy to forget that the need for company is one of the strongest driving forces they possess.

The difference between a horse alone and a horse in company is often pathetically great. When Septem first came to us, he had hardly been handled at all, and I felt that before turning him out in the paddock with the others it would be wise to get him used to man and to the feel of a head-collar inside the stables. For the first twenty-four hours he stood in the loose-box quite quietly. His initial response on being approached was to lay back his ears and strike out with his forefeet, but after some hours of being fed, petted and handled, he abandoned this reaction and stood motionless at our approach, with a sullen stare. During this time the other stables were empty, the horses being at grass, and Septem was to all intents and purposes alone. However, during the course of his second day with us we brought two of the other horses

38

in to prepare them for a ride, turning them out again later. Septem had been thrilled at their proximity, but after their departure he turned suddenly into a raving maniac. He pawed the door and kept rearing up in an attempt to jump out, so that in order to prevent him from hurting himself it was necessary to shut the stable entirely. The only light and air that entered it now came from a small window 4 ft. 6 ins. from the ground. Before long there was a splintering of glass, and one of Septem's forefeet appeared through the window, covered with blood. He extricated himself without serious damage, but continued to thrash about inside the box, threatening to make a second attempt. To prevent this, I tied him to a ring in the wall, but this restriction only seemed to aggravate him further. He tore at the rope, broke innumerable head-collars, banged his head and flanks incessantly against the walls, and was as often as not off his legs altogether. His reaction to us now was entirely different. No longer did he either strike out or stand stubbornly mute. At our approach he would prick his ears, nuzzle our hands, and push his head forward to have it stroked. So long as there was someone beside him, the hysterical antics would be stilled, only to start again the moment he was left alone. He was not calmed until finally one of the other horses was brought in to stand next door. Then, within a few seconds, Septem was transformed. This is not to say that he became a docile, tractable animal within a moment, but at least the raving maniac was stilled and a fairly rational animal returned to being one which could eat, drink, and stand looking intelligently out on to the world without trying to break everything within sight.

The effect of social deprivation, particularly in youth, has been studied systematically over a period of fifteen years or more by Harlow and his colleagues in the United States.[12]

Using monkeys as his 'guinea pigs' and removing these from their mothers immediately they were born, Harlow raised the infants in states of partial deprivation on 'surrogate' mothers made of wire, but supplying either milk or a warm cloth covering or both milk and cuddliness.

It was found, as expected, that deprivation during infancy

39

of companionship, food or comfort had a detrimental effect on the sexual and maternal behaviour of the adult; but what was perhaps even more surprising to most people was that removal of the comforting cuddliness of the surrogate mother's cloth covering had a more serious effect than shortage of food, and that complete social isolation produced an adult that was incapable of responding adequately to any sort of normal situation, not just one involving other members of the species. In other words the adult behaved as if mentally defective and not just socially retarded.

Harlow then began re-introducing stimuli to his deprived subjects to discover what the important minimal environment was that would forestall such disaster. The general finding was again surprising. It seemed that the isolated youngster only had to see other members of its own species for quite short periods and at quite infrequent intervals for the effect of complete social deprivation to be avoided; but—and this is one of the important points which will be referred to again in Chapter II—the age at which this 'visual stimulation' took place was crucial. If the monkey was not quite young at the time it first saw another monkey, the stimulation had no effect at all.

Another important aspect of social behaviour whose importance has come to be recognized in recent years, is the effect of different species on one another. It has long been realized that if a young animal of one species is fostered by another, the youngster will grow up to identify more closely with the foster species than with its own. Bucket reared lambs will follow their milk dispensing foster-mothers for months in preference to joining their herds. The fact that even mature social animals prefer any living company to none at all is less often appreciated, and yet as just described Septem showed just this.

This does not mean to say that horses are not very choosy among themselves and are capable of intense and individual likes and dislikes. The high-spirited Swanny, for instance, became very much enamoured of my grey mare, Quattor. She was most resentful when, in view of the damage she was doing to all her companions, I put her in a separate field with a less valuable fellow, and she spent most of her time craning over the intervening hedge, letting out viciously whenever the gelding with her approached too near.

Such attachments often seem to be rather one-sided, and passion on the part of one may continue despite endless rebuffs from the other. When I first arrived at Stones Farm I only had two horses, Unus, the old bay, and the mettlesome four-year-old chestnut mare, Secunda. Unus soon became devoted to Secunda and paid her more serious attention than I had ever seen him show to anything, either before or after. After some weeks together, they were joined by the little roan pony, Peter. Now Peter was a most possessive and aggressive character. Although barely 13-hands, he had the dominance and will-power of many small beings, and soon bulldozed his way over Unus and usurped the mare. Unus, who has never been known to kick or fight, moved sadly away, and within half an hour of Peter's arrival the pony and Secunda were standing under one clump of trees whisking the flies off one another, while poor old Unus was standing fifty yards away beneath another. After some weeks of this ménage I had expected Unus' ardour to have cooled somewhat, but not a bit. If he was taken out of the field away from his beloved—or, even more surprisingly, if she were taken away, leaving him and Peter together—Unus behaved as if bereft. Peter in the meantime showed the impassivity of one who knows perfectly well that his lady will be true to him no matter where she is. He would wait contentedly until Secunda returned and then firmly but decisively reclaim her as his own.

Later on, after Tertia's arrival, Unus and she became quite good friends, although Unus showed none of the passion for her with which he had pursued Secunda. Unfortunately, Tertia could be a little minx on occasion, and she never hesitated to kick out if in the mood to do so. One day I was taking her and Unus to a meet in the trailer which until then had been used without a centre partition. We had not gone three miles along the road before the car was nearly thrown off the road by bumps and lurches from behind. On stopping to see what was the matter, I found Unus sweating and

41

panting and rolling his eyes, with one hind leg in the air, while Tertia stared about her innocently. I could see nothing wrong from in front and was about to put down the ramp to investigate further when Tertia suddenly laid back her ears and kicked sideways, catching Unus on his already nearly broken leg with enough force to knock him over. While we were struggling to get the ramp down and before we could get Tertia away, she had kicked Unus a third time, and when we did finally get her out the poor old horse was trembling like a leaf, with blood pouring from him.

One might have expected him to be only too glad to be rid of such a travelling companion, but the moment he was alone Unus started calling to Tertia as if his heart would break. While I was turning the trailer, he pounded up and down, and when we passed Tertia on the way home he nearly broke the door in his efforts to return to her.

That this is not an isolated or particularly abnormal instance was shown later on by another scene between Septem and Octavius. These two had always appeared to be fairly good friends, although there was a definite under-standing between them that Septem was the boss. Only Octavius, Septem and Quinque occupied the fields at the time of which I am writing, and Quinque was definitely Septem's girl. One night Octavius and Quinque had been brought in for their evening feeds and were not put out again until after dark. It appeared that, unknown to us, and before their return to the paddock, Septem had jumped out of the field to look for them and later on spent the night in a neighbouring paddock. When I went to put him back in the morning, he was extremely tiresome. It had been raining hard all night, and the horses were all very wild. None of them would let me get a rope or halter round their necks, and although Septem would dash up to the fence separating him from the others he would neither jump it now of his own accord nor wait by the gate till I had opened it for him. Octavius, in the meantime, grew very agitated and made repeated attempts to get out to Septem as if to protect him from me. He was most resentful of Quinque joining in the fun and would lay his ears back at her every time she came too close to him. When finally the three were reunited, all the recompense Octavius received for his faithfulness and devotion was to be set upon by Septem and chased round the field away from Quinque. Every time the mare moved away from his side a few inches, Septem would renew his unprovoked and unwarranted charges, chivvying poor Octavius far into the afternoon.

However, despite the violence and antagonism which two horses may show towards one another in one setting, they may react very differently in another. Peter was fiendish to Unus at home and, as has been mentioned, would chase him away from Secunda with ferocity. But when Peter and Unus were taken out hunting or to a gymkhana together they could not bear to be parted from one another for a second without calling and fussing as if they had been the best of friends for life. Such behaviour, with its sympathies and antipathies, is sometimes difficult to understand.

Although horses react to the presence of a live companion with such violent demonstrations of affection or distaste, they seem curiously insensitive to the pain and even death of their fellows.

The night that Nona died, in agonies from a twisted gut, I was much too concerned over her welfare to bother about Unus and Nuts in their adjoining boxes. It was only later that I was able to marvel at the calm unconcern with which they had continued to munch throughout the tragic drama. Even when Unus peered over his door in the morning at the cold body stretched out in the straw beside him, he seemed peculiarly unmoved and stared only in curiosity at the distress to which I myself gave vent every time I thought of it. Yet only a few hours earlier he had been raving up and down the field as one bereft when the same horse had been taken from his company to be shod.

Once before I had been struck by a similar lack of sensitivity and sentimentality in horses. During the war several horses were evacuated to me in Wales. One of them, an elderly thoroughbred 'chaser who was in poor condition when he arrived, was obviously most unsuited to spend any winter in the open, let alone to stand the intense and prolonged cold which we experienced during 1940 in the Welsh hills. Despite every effort, the poor animal gradually grew weaker until one day he was unable to get up out of the snow which had frozen around him overnight. As a last attempt to save him, I surrounded him with hay and straw, hoping that he would warm up enough to be able to get to his feet and make the inside of some stable. He did not, and the only thing to do was to hasten his inevitable end. While I was waiting for the knackers to arrive, and frequently giving vent to my own grief, I was horrified to see the other horses calmly picking over the hay and straw which surrounded the body of their companion, as if the latter had little more significance to them than an unsightly sack.

It seems to be only among the higher animals that the concept of death brings unhappiness. During the bitterly cold winter of 1947 I was engaged on some experimental work with monkeys, and because the monkey house was the only building in Oxford at that time which had been allowed to keep its central heating on, I spent considerably more time with my charges, and consequently got to know them rather better, than I might otherwise have done.

During the course of these experiments new monkeys were continually arriving, and one day there appeared in the house two charming little newcomers, aged about nine months. Like shy children in a new school, they crouched huddled up together in the corner of their cage, unwilling to respond to any of our overtures or accept our offerings. For far longer than usual they maintained this aloofness. They seemed to be sufficient unto themselves and to find all the companionship they needed in one another. Unfortunately, one of the pair had contracted tuberculosis on the voyage over and died within a few weeks of its arrival. For days the other was inconsolable. Despite the presence of would-be comforters all around and above it, it remained distraught and pitiful, sobbing in the corner of its cage with its head in its arms like a small baby. Every time the door of the monkey-house opened it jumped up hopefully, peering towards the entrance through red-rimmed eyes from which the big tears dripped down its nose and cheeks. No human has ever mourned a

44

personal friend more genuinely and pathetically.

Despite their attitude to those that are dead, horses will always behave unitedly and as a herd the moment there is any question of danger. For this reason some people regard the herd instinct, or gregariousness, as primarily a method of self-protection. It is argued that if animals which have to spend much of their time eating, like horses, had always to be on the look-out as well, their constitutions and digestions would necessarily suffer. By moving around in herds the job of look-out can be shared so that each one has a turn to eat his fill. Whether this is so or not I do not know, but I have certainly noticed that when several horses are together they do seem to take turns to keep watch. In the day-time it is rare to see all the horses of a group lying down together. One is almost always on the look-out and even if he appears to be asleep will react to the slightest sound or movement with amazing alacrity. Interestingly enough, this habit seems to persist even among horses in the stables. During our nightly vigils at Stones Farm (about which more will be said later on) we noticed that as one of the stabled horses got up another would lie down, and as he in turn got up the first would go back to sleep again. Among some other animals, such as red deer, the job of look-out seems to be confined to a few responsible members of the community, and is not shared equally by all; probably the same holds for horses. Those at Stones Farm who were most often on the alert and acting as sentinels at night were the greys, Quattuor and Octavius. In view of the fact that they could be seen by intending enemies, or others, from far greater distances than the darker coloured horses, they probably had need for this atten-tiveness—a need which has been foreseen and taken care of by nature. Alertness, however, did not necessarily signify dominance, and it would have been a mistake to imagine from Octavius' restlessness and the way in which he rounded up his companions in the dark that he was the boss of the group. In some respects, as already mentioned, he was firmly kept in place by Septem and did not dare to approach a mare while Septem was in the vicinity. The tradition of the 'lordly white stallion of the prairies' may have its origin in the same

45

phenomenon. The animal seen against the sky-line snorting and pawing the ground may be the keen-eyed self-appointed sentinel and not necessarily the leader.

Whatever the actual functions and origins of herd behaviour, however, it is necessary for animals which are going to live together in a crowd to adapt their behaviour in certain ways. It is necessary for them to have a social structure—that is to say, a code of laws and morals to which all agree to adhere. At one time it was believed that most animal societies were built on a hierarchical system, the grades of which are often far more rigid and clearly defined than the Victorian social distinctions in England. Hens are a classical example. Among all confined communities of these birds it will be found that one is top-dog and can peck all the others, while one is the under-dog and can be pecked by the rest. Lorenz[26] studied a jackdaw community raised on his own roof and found much the same situation developing among them, with, however, some interesting differences. When two jackdaws mate they do so for life, and the female automatically adopts the hierarchy of the male she mates with. If a high-grade cock decides to court and become engaged to a hen very much below him in rank, not only is the new wife immediately raised to his own status, but as she assumes her new position she may become far more aggressive to those who were previously her superiors than if she had been born to the aristocracy.

In the majority of animals, however, including horses, the pattern is seldom followed so exactly. A major difficulty in assessing an individual's position in the hierarchy is to decide the criteria to be used in measurement. Threats or gestures of anger would seem the obvious ones, but in fact these might be very misleading. It is not always the horse which gets what it wants most easily that has to make the greatest number of threats in order to do so. In my own time I have had two very dominant mares: in each case when out in a field with other horses, the mare had only to flick an ear or quiver her tail for all her companions to flee.

When threats were made, it was usually observed that each individual tended to pick on one or two others for special

46

attention, as if deciding that these were his or her particular rivals and that the others did not count. By using threats as his criterion for measurement, Montgomery,[29] who studied ten horses for a total of fourteen hours (divided into twelve periods), found that 'triangular' relationships as well as uni-directional relationships had to be accepted: that was to say A threatened B who threatened C who in turn threatened A. Tyler[37] felt that in the semi-wild New Forest ponies, rank order within the small (family) groups had to be distinguished from that in other groups. Several of these family groups consisting of a mother and her daughters might join up together to form larger groups which shared the same home range. Within the family the rank order was fairly strict and linear and depended on age, but within the larger group, the offspring of a dominant mare often assumed the dam's dominance, and rank order became extremely complicated.

The tendency for family members to stick together and to form special relationships with one another has been noted by many private (or small) breeders, but exceptions have also been found. In my own experience, mares find their offspring as different (and often problematical!) as many human mothers. One of the first brood mares I had, a grey three-quarter thoroughbred, Nuki, was particularly antipathetic to her own daughters. The oldest of these, Nauri, and the second, Nuit, had both inherited many of her own characteristics, and when mature like their mother took a poor view of playing second fiddle to anyone. Perhaps it was for this reason that Nuki saw them as her greatest dangers and felt the need to keep them under her thumb. Her sons and grandsons, however, were very seldom threatened. Although she would not let her daughters come within five or six yards of her when she was waiting to go through a gate or resting in the shade, she would allow her sons to lean on her without turning a hair.

The sons, however, had their own special friends and enemies. Gwilliam was one of Nuki's grandsons, his father being Nuki's son Gamesman and his dam a Welsh cob. Gwilliam only came into my possession at three years of age and having not been given any special care when young was much smaller than most of my other horses at that age. He was even smaller than the only other gelding I had on the place at the time, Giggle, a two-year-old also by Gamesman out of a rather retiring thoroughbred mare. As soon as Gwilliam arrived, however, he took possession of the place, his special rival being Giggle. Although threats were occasionally levelled at some of the mares, none of them received anything like the same sort of attention.

Threats vary in number and intensity according to place and occupation. It has been noticed among ponies in the Camargue[9] that young mares which wanted to join a herd of older ones would be accepted by the latter, while they were all moving from place to place, or grazing, but not while they were resting. In the same way the 'individual distance' (i.e. the distance one animal will allow another to approach it before threatening) between Nuki and one of her daughters was smaller in the centre of the field than near the gate.

Two of the most important factors in determining individual distance appear to be (1) competition; and (2) danger. Although it might seem that these could be identical on occasion (danger meaning competition for security) they tend in fact to have the opposite effects. Danger brings individuals together in the same way that it does Mankind. Individual rivalries are forgotten: ideas of 'the common good' are re-aroused. Even rival groups will join up in flight from the supposed enemy. The urge to join company on these occasions is so great that a frightened horse will make for others even though, in order to reach them, it may have to pass close to the very thing that is frightening it. There is a large meadow outside Oxford on which a number of horses used to be turned out. In this meadow it was quite common for groups of horses which were particularly friendly to separate out and graze together in small bands and these bands could often be found in the same place day after day. As soon as danger was signalled there would be a general rushing together of all the isolated bands, and social prestige appeared to be forgotten in the desire for personal safety. Moreover, if one little band saw another on the move it immediately suspected the worst and joined in the rush, and in next to no time there would be a general stampede. It was only necessary to make one free horse trot a few paces on Port Meadow for all 100 to gallop madly and purposelessly the best part of two miles.

I once observed a most amusing instance of this, the originator being a small foal, who nearly suffered seriously himself as a consequence. The foal's pony mother belonged to a herd of about fifteen. She and another, whose sex I did not notice but who was behaving rather like a possessive aunt, were feeding a few yards from the rest, while the foal scampered and gallivanted at their side. As the herd fed on, it passed about fifty yards from a small knoll. In one of its scurries the foal found the foot of this knoll and delightedly went back to its mother with the news. It immediately left her side again and returned to its find, this time scampering a little higher up on the knoll before returning. No sooner had it reached its mother's side the second time than it was off again, and on this occasion surmounted the knoll's top. There, proud and pleased, it stayed, while mother evidently to see what her child was up to, began walking over towards it. After she had gone a few paces the possessive aunt suddenly seemed to realize that she was being left out and began to trot after the mother. One of the main bunch noticed her movement and started off at a canter after the aunt. In no time at all the entire herd was making for this knoll at top speed, while other small bands, awakened by the rush, joined in from the vicinity. Seeing the oncoming mob, the foal turned tail and bolted, mother, aunt and crowd fast on its heels and quickly overtaking it. As they disappeared into the distance I saw the foal beginning to drop behind, exhausted, its mother urging it on to keep up in the pointless gallop.

While every small herd of horses appears to find a leader among its community, there seem to be some animals which will maintain their dominance or submissiveness whatever the company they are in. Unus was invariably submissive. Much as he adored Secunda, he did not fight an inch to get her back from Peter. If he ever kicked out, he always made sure there was no one within reach. His kicks, unlike those of

49

some horses, were tokens, not intentions. After Peter left, Billy Bunter came to join our community, and once again Unus relinquished his transitory possession of the mares to the new gelding. In the kicking hierarchy Unus was always at the bottom. After a summer out at grass in company he was one mass of cuts, bruises, scratches and tooth-marks, while others remained unscathed. Billy Bunter, on the contrary, was indisputably a leader and boss. During his stay at Stones Farm no other gelding was allowed near the mares until they had accepted his position and were prepared to play second fiddle. His place was taken after his departure by Septem, a gelding of very similar temperament and physique who, despite his youth, had not been at Stones Farm for more than a couple of weeks before he too was dictator.

But what happens when two domineering types come together? The answer is probably never predictable but has to be worked out by the individuals. We had one interesting—if rather unpleasant—example of this at Stones Farm, from which I learned always to think very carefully before ever buying a new horse, and to consider just how its temperament was going to fit in with those of the animals already there. The situation in question arose when Septem, Billy Bunter and Peter, the three successive tyrants, were all at Stones Farm together for a brief period. The occasion was that of a local gymkhana, for which Peter and Billy (under his new ownership) had been ridden over by their owners to stay the night. Billy immediately tried to return to his previous position as leader of the herd, now occupied by Septem, but the latter stood his ground and refused to be pushed over. Their fights looked like being so furious and disastrous that we did our best to keep them apart in different fields. However, they apparently enjoyed their scraps no less than many humans do theirs and refused to have their fun upset. At first we put Billy with one of the mares into one paddock and Peter by himself in another, leaving Septem with Unus and two others in a third field. However, Billy, who had previously been schooled over the fences adjoining these different fields, skipped from one to the other without care or trouble, closely pursued by an

50

enraged and blundering Septem, who carried all our beautiful fences with him. Having repaired a little of the damage, we tried putting Septem out with one of the mares, leaving Billy with Unus and the rest; but this did not satisfy them either. They both wanted all, and were not going to be content with a mere share of the company. Before we had finished patching up one fence there would be a gap in another, and Billy and Septem would once more be at it hammer and tongs. Their battles went on unceasingly far into the night, their kicks mingling horribly out of the darkness with squeals, thuds and grunts. By some miracle no serious injury was done, but as, after twelve hours, neither had been declared the winner or showed any sign of giving way to the other, I decided that, much as I would have liked to continue observing the situation and watch its outcome, human intervention was necessary to avoid tragedy. Billy was removed and kept in a closed stable until his owner could ride him away, when peace once more returned.

During this time Unus and, even more curiously, Peter, had both shown complete indifference to the situation. Neither had made any attempt to join in the scuffles or to usurp the mares when these were temporarily neglected. It is true that Peter had been put in a field by himself, but his isolation was continually being disrupted and his territory infringed by the contestants. Nevertheless, he remained aloof and immobile, watching them from a distance. Occasionally he would lay back his ears at Unus if the latter came too close to him over the fence, but he seemed to realize that others were present with a right to dominance over him and he put up no opposition.

Although the gregarious tendencies of horses have so far only been considered in relation to their behaviour when free, they may in reality have many more far-reaching consequences and implications of interest to those who ride. May it not be possible, for instance, that kickers are the naturally dominant types? If this is so, then obviously beating a horse for kicking is unlikely to cure it of the habit. In fact, it will probably only make it worse, for a domineering horse will only kick at another if the latter tries

51

to come too close to it. If the kicker is beaten every time it kicks, it will naturally come to associate the beating with the proximity of other horses and so kick all the harder to keep the others at bay. However, once a horse has come to realize that riding groups are not natural herds and that when under the saddle he is under the dominance of his rider, then the habit of kicking may be dropped, whether the horse has previously been beaten for it or not.

There is one aspect of some horses' behaviour which can only be understood in the light of their normal tendency to keep with others. This is napping. When a horse naps, it is trying to get back either to its stable (its own home territory, where it will feel safe) or to other horses. The urge to join company on these occasions is so great that a frightened horse will make for others even though, in order to reach them, it may have to pass closer to the very thing that is frightening it. A friend and I were walking across Port Meadow one day when we found ourselves in the centre of a small grazing herd whose members continued to feed, despite our presence, without lifting their heads. After a few seconds I withdrew a little way and left my friend in the centre of the peaceful scene, armed, however, with a white scarf and a large rattle. At a word of command she transformed herself from a peace-loving citizen into a spectacle sufficient to put fear into the heart of the bravest and most sophisticated pony. Raising her scarf and rattle over her head, she began waving them hard and shouting at the top of her voice. Immediately, all the horses leapt away, some in one direction and some in another. It looked for a moment as though the herd was to be split up and disintegrate, but after a few seconds those which were going off to the right stopped in their tracks, swung round, and with heads tucked in and tails aloft charged back, passing within a few feet of my friend, her scarf and her rattle, to join up with the others.

Now although horses always like to be in the proximity of others they will only rush for company in the way just described if discomfited or in danger. When peacefully grazing a horse will frequently wander some distance from the herd without worrying. This fact suggests that napping is only motivated by fear and a lack of confidence in the world at large. The happy, satisfied, confident riding horse, like the one that is eating with a peaceful mind, will walk or gallop away from its companions without objection. But any horse—even the quietest and most docile—may turn nappy if truly frightened. This fact was brought home to me very forcibly a little while ago when I was schooling a young horse for a friend. The horse had reached a stage when he would pop over low but solid pieces of timber without worrying and appeared to enjoy jumping. Indeed, he went on later to become a very successful competitor in One- and Three-day Events; but one afternoon during these early days I decided to take the guard rail away from in front of one fence—a single pole—in order that the horse should not become too dependent on its presence. At the first attempt the horse misjudged everything and blundered badly into the pole. When faced at the fence a second time he was clearly much upset, rushed headlong at it, and again sent the obstacle flying. When I remounted after collecting and re-erecting the debris, the horse suddenly, and for the first time since I had ridden him, bolted for the gate leading to his stable-yard. Moreover, I had the greatest difficulty in persuading him later to return anywhere near the scene of his shame. Every few yards he would stop, swing round, and make back for his yard. He had, in short, suddenly become nappy, and it was necessary to put the guard rail back in front of the fence and coax him quietly over this several times more to regain his confidence before his faith was restored and his nappiness disappeared.

From these considerations it is obvious that beatings, shooings, cursings—in fact, all the usual ruses employed to stop horses from napping—will only worsen the condition instead of improving it, since they only serve to decrease the animal's confidence in the outside world. We found this to be the case with Billy Bunter, who was extremely nappy when I first got him. In view of his bumptiousness and friendliness when approached on foot, this was at first difficult to understand, but one day I happened to mount him while I was holding a stick. The usually stolid, self-willed fat boy suddenly became a shivering jelly. As I was fiddling about for my stirrups, he tucked himself up and dashed off as if he had been hit, while for a long time after I had stopped him and tried to soothe him he continued to jump as if expecting the worst every time I moved. On another occasion I was getting ready to put him at a small fence which he knew well and jumped willingly, when I pulled together the ends of my reins and let them drop down on the side of his neck. The movement had been unconsidered and unintentional on my part, but it was the same movement which might well have been made had I been gathering up the reins to slap his neck with them. Again Billy shot forward, with his ears back, as if prepared for a good hiding. After these experiences it was not difficult to understand why it took some weeks of continuous patting and reassurance to persuade Billy to leave other horses and go away on his own.

The length of time over which a pattern of behaviour may persist in some horses once it has been established—and the ease with which it can be elicited again after it has been eradicated—are often quite surprising. Only very intimate knowledge of an individual spaced over many years can explain certain of his mannerisms. This was first brought home to me by His Nibs, Nuki's third foal. When I decided to put a head-collar on him for the first time, I was without regular stable help and decided to try the job single-handed. While Nuki's attention was occupied with a bowl of oats I slipped one arm over His Nibs' neck and the front of the foal-slip over his nose. His Nibs stood quite quietly while I got this far but as soon as he felt the straps tighten over the back of his poll he began backing away at a rate of knots. Hard as I tried to keep up with him he finally slipped the rope out of my hand and ran away loose. It was some time before I managed to recapture him and tried to lead him once again. Again, as soon as he felt the pull of the headcollar on his head he began backing away fast and it was a long time before I was able to catch up with him and stop him. After that, once he had learned that being held on a head-collar was no trouble, His Nibs was very easy to manage. Indeed, unlike many of Nuki's offspring he could always be controlled by a piece of light rope on a head-collar however high he jumped or however much on his toes he might be. However, the tendency to go backwards when in doubt remained his own special form of dealing with unpleasant phenomena, and recurred three years later when I began putting the tackle on him to break him in.

The extent to which a horse's first reactions to a situation can be used to predict how it will behave later on is doubtful. Guessing Game ('Guss') and Noisette ('Netta'), both of whom were bred at Leyland Farm, illustrate this point well. Netta was Nuki's fifth foal and Guss was Nuki's grandson, by Gamesman out of a very nervous and accident-prone mare, Whose Lady. Guss, unlike Netta, was extremely apprehensive of anything new but once it became apparent to him that it did not hurt he was prepared to accept it from then on and give it no further thought. Netta, on the other hand, although unafraid of anything new, very often played up for the sake of seeing what response she would elicit; and once she had decided that a certain thing was to be shied at she would continue shying at it for many weeks. Guss and Netta were taken to their first Show together: where Guss was expected to provide the trouble while Netta was expected to be perfectly placid. However, when it came to the point these rôles were completely reversed. Guss, although he came out of the horsebox like a champagne cork and did several circles on his hind legs, soon settled down to accept his lot. Netta began comparatively quietly but gradually excitement built up in her. Just as the other youngsters were beginning to settle down, she erupted and began whirling round on her hind legs. Moreover, while Netta at home had always gone quietly and easily into the horsebox whereas Guss had been very difficult to persuade to enter it, it was Guss who led up the steep ramp at the show while Netta had to be pushed in behind him.

I made a similar mistake in my predictions when Gamesman himself was a foal and was taken to his first Show together with his stable companion of that time, a little Welsh yearling colt Peregrine. When being trained to lead at home it was Peregrine who gave the early trouble. While

Gamesman would lumber along good naturedly but rather clumsily doing all he was told, Peregrine would be dancing around first on one pair of legs, then on the other. At the Show it was Gamesman who was expected to behave himself and Peregrine to cause a disturbance; but once in the unfamiliar setting it was in fact Gamesman who gave all the trouble, while Peregrine gave the impression of being 'the perfect child's pony'.

The examples of social interaction which have been given here, as well as others which might be quoted, afford ample evidence that there exists among horses a code or language by which the social structure of the herd is maintained. But how do horses get to know the code? How do they communicate with one another?

It has often been maintained that language is the prerogative of man. It is true that so far as we are able to make out no other animals appear to be capable of communicating abstract concepts to one another in the same way as we can do, but this may primarily be due to their inability to grasp abstract concepts at all and is not necessarily due to defects of communication. It has in fact been established that most animals are able to communicate with one another and that much of their behaviour depends on the presence of signals given and received by individuals. These signals sometimes consist of movements, sometimes of sounds, and sometimes of smells, and it is often difficult to know what aspect of an animal's total behaviour constitutes a signal and what part of it is just coincidental. In the case of horses, however, there are already several well known signs and signals. A snort signifies a warning of danger to the whole herd. A whinny stands for pleasure. Ears back means 'look out', and if the tail is lashed as well it means that a kick will probably follow. It needs a great deal of careful observation to find out the true basis of different animal languages, but that the time and energy spent on this is often well rewarded has been shown in several instances. Von Frisch's discovery of the language of the honey bee and Lorenz's discovery of duck language are interesting examples.[27,38]

Recent studies of communication in horses has mainly

been confined to analysing the different sounds they make[21], [40], [30], but most observers are coming to the conclusion that sounds are less significant than are muscular movements or gestures. It is true that most horses will recognize and respond very quickly to an alarm call—a snort of fear or a 'where are you' neigh—and that many nursing mothers are able to pick out the calls of their own offspring from those of other foals. The signals which seem to keep order within the herd, however, are largely gestural, and there is some evidence that these have to be learned by the individuals concerned. Early in the 1970's a veterinary neighbour of mine experimented with a method of rearing orphaned or rejected foals on an automatic calf-suckling machine which dispensed milk on demand, rather like the wire surrogate mother of Harlow's monkeys. The first foals so raised bore an even closer similarity to Harlow's monkeys, in that they had been brought up isolated from their own species; and it was very striking that when they were put with other horses not only did they appear unable to communicate with the others, but the others showed little interest in them except to tease or chase them.

Most young horses will approach an older horse with movements of their teeth and mouth commonly referred to as 'snapping'. The gesture, however, far from being one of threat is really one of submission or appeasement rather similar to the grin of a dog or even a human. It is a very powerful inhibition of anger, and no adult horse in a normal social situation would attack another horse which greeted it with this sign. This gesture appears to be inborn in that some foals will 'snap' when approached by any large object within an hour or two of birth. Gradually most foals 'learn' the animals towards which the gesture is relevant, and they do not snap except in the presence of an older member of their own species. The socially deprived foals, however, never or only very belatedly learned the value of the snapping gesture and would often continue to snap to a human while failing to do so to another horse.[49]

Other signals which may have particular significance to horses are conveyed by touch. Mutual grooming or wither-nibbling is part of an elaborate social ritual.

Most of the signals which have been described up to now are of a more or less automatic character. That is to say that they are made by the giver spontaneously in response to particular situations and evoke spontaneous, unlearned (and even uncontrollable) responses from those that receive them. They are similar to laughter and tears in us. The question of whether horses, or, for that matter, any other animals have an acquired language as well as this automatic one still awaits a definite answer. It has been maintained that some kinds of birds have an acquired language as well as an inborn one, and that the songs of individuals within a species may vary quite a lot in different localities. Thus although in general a jackdaw raised in Russia understands and responds to the cries of an Austrian jackdaw, significant nuances in the signals of birds from one locality may pass unnoticed by those from another. It is as if all were born with knowledge of the basic language but develop different dialects as well.[26]

If this occurs in birds it probably occurs in many other species, and many of the misunderstandings seen among individuals of the same species in the animal world may be due to the wrong interpretation being given to signals. That there *are* individual differences in the way horses give and respond to signals we know already, but whether these reflect merely the idiosyncracies of character or whether they are due to social influences it is difficult to say. Just as no two people smile in exactly the same way, so no two horses whinny alike. Just as no two people read the same message in a smile, so no two horses respond to a signal in identical ways. When one hears a warning snort, he will trot off a few paces and then turn round to see what threatens; another will have a look first and then trot off. If one horse lays back its ears and swings round its quarters, some, like Unus and Octavius, will move out of reach; others, like Septem and Billy Bunter, will try to get their kicks in first.

While many of these differences are undoubtedly due to experience and upbringing, other differences may well be hereditary.

Among the horses which I myself have bred, reared and final-

58

ly broken-in, there have been a number of cases in which a pattern of behaviour typical of one parent has suddenly appeared in its offspring. Gambit was especially interesting to me as he was the first horse I bred whose dam and sire were both well known to me. Gambit's dam, called Muffin the Mule by her stable connections (Muff for short) was a bitterly disappointing mare whose appearance and abilities (she was fast and a superb jumper when she liked to be) were both top class. She should have been everybody's dream of a middle-weight hunter. To ride, however, she had two serious shortcomings: (1) a tendency to buck in a most unseating manner (one shoulder would suddenly vanish from underneath the rider and at the same time she would screw herself round to one side); and (2) a tendency to shy at traffic. The latter is one of the worst faults a modern horse can have, for even on the smallest country lanes it is possible to meet cars and lorries going at high speeds and occupying all except a few yards of the road's width; and a horse which is not prepared to stand quite still while they pass can easily cause a fatality. Muff was nine years old when I bought her (primarily as a brood mare) and by then her two tendencies were both deeply ingrained. How they had originated I had no idea but one thing I did decide after a very short time was that neither I nor anyone else for whom I was responsible was going to continue riding her. Even as a brood mare she proved disappointing to begin with. It was two years before she became pregnant, and this was only achieved by turning her out with Gamesman (he was then just two years old) and letting him chase and chivvy her till she gave in to him. Gamesman himself had been known to me since he was born; and every one of his various maturational stages had been carefully plotted.

The product of this union, Gambit, was born with difficulty, and for the first three years of his life remained a comic, stunted little figure of fun. When first broken and backed he quickly showed that he had his mother's temper as well as her potential abilities; but he resisted all temptations to buck till quite suddenly on one occasion when he was particularly irritated, he dropped his shoulder and screwed round to one side in a complete replica of his dam's action. Fortunately for him as well as for his riders, he did not resort to this action very often, but when it did so it was usually a winner.

The first time I rode Gambit in traffic I took him out by himself early one Sunday morning soon after he had been broken in. We did not meet any traffic until we haad been going for nearly half-an-hour and until he had already spent a good deal of his energy in shying and snorting at other things. By the time we met our first vehicle he seemed resigned to the fact that the world was a crazy place, and walked past the car without a qualm. 'It is reassuring to find', I wrote in my diary that day, 'that Gambit has not inherited his mother's reaction to traffic'. Gambit was sold the following year, and two years later I went to see how he was getting on in his new home. By that time he had already made a name for himself as a Show jumper and Event horse and was receiving all the love and care possible. 'He only has one fault' said his owner 'and that is traffic. Quite honestly I don't dare take him out on the roads now if there is a chance of meeting lorries. If he doesn't turn and bolt he stands and shakes with fear.'

One other instance of an unfortunate behaviour tendency apparently being inherited was from Samantha, another mare that I bought to breed from after she had achieved maturity. Samantha was out at grass when I bought her, and it was not till she had already produced her first foal that she was brought into the stable, where it turned out that she was a 'weaver' (weaving is the action of standing with the head over the stable door or gate and swinging the head and body from side to side putting the weight first on one foot and then on the other. It is usually regarded as a sign of tension or boredom, and because such horses are difficult to keep fit, is regarded as a stable vice). Although Samantha did not weave out at grass, she was so bad in the stable that I was not surprised when her first foal seemed to have caught it off her, and also began weaving when stabled. When Samantha had her second foal, I was therefore very careful never to keep her in the stable with it. If she and the foal had to be under cover they were put in a large yard where the mare's habit was less likely to be aroused. This foal, Gimmick, (another son of Gamesman) seemed consequently to have escaped the weaving habit, and was sold when he was three years old in all good faith as 'free from all stable vices'. Free he remained for the first few weeks in his new home, when to the horror of everyone he began to weave. Although the habit with him was never firmly established, he often began to weave if he was kept shut up in a small stable for any length of time.

CURIOSITY

In many of the text-books on horses, curiosity is mentioned as one of their basic instincts. It is true that instances of curiosity can often be seen among horses, and they therefore deserve especial attention.

But if we drop the word 'instinct' as suggested at the beginning of this Chapter, how are we to deal with curiosity? It is hardly a need, nor an urge, nor is it exactly a pattern of behaviour.

Curiosity seems rather to be a name used to describe a certain type of reaction, a name which probably camouflages its true origins and mechanisms and thereby gives a false sense of understanding. After all, it does not really matter what an act is called. What is important is that we should know how an act arises, what causes it, and how it functions.

In order to discover this, it is easiest to study a few concrete examples, noting in particular when and in what situations they occur. Most people will be able to think of instances from their own experience. A young horse is walking down a road and stops suddenly, with ears pricked, looking at a pile of white stones on the roadside. At first he tries to shy away, but if we are firm and keep him from evading the issue, he will probably put down his head and walk forward to sniff at it. Why does he do this, and why, when he is a little older and has investigated many such piles, does he then pass them by without bothering?

The instances of curiosity in horses which stand out most clearly in my own memory are concerned with their behaviour when loose in our own paddocks. Tertia was full of fun and games, but although very friendly to anyone so long as they were on their feet, it took us many weeks to persuade her to tolerate a rider on her back. During the time she was being broken in, she was living out, and whenever we went into her paddock she would follow us around as if glued to our heels. The moment a coat, bucket, saddle or bridle was placed on the ground she would start sniffing and nibbling it like a dog. At this time we were occupied in taking down a wire fence between two paddocks and replacing it with wooden rails. The operation necessitated banging in many stakes with sledge-hammers. Tertia behaved as if the whole process was being carried out for her especial benefit. After trampling on our coats and upsetting the box of nails she would come up to the stake on which we were working and hold her nose a few inches from its top, scarcely flinching as the heavy (and not very expertly wielded) head slammed down a few inches from her whiskers. Everything that went on in the fields at this time was grist to her mill and had to be investigated. Sad to say that later on, when she became more experienced and amenable to bring ridden, this rather engaging characteristic faded.

Septem was another pony who showed many of Tertia's traits, including her almost insatiable curiosity, during the course of his training. I have already described how at one time Septem was extremely difficult to catch and appeared to regard all humans as potential dangers. During this period we found to our cost that it was fatal to leave any precious object unattended within his reach. As soon as we had gone ten paces from it, it would be trampled and chewed beyond repair.

But the most outstanding and revealing instance of curiosity concerned the arrival of Betsy, our pig. The dislike and suspicion of pigs shown by many horses is notorious, and ours were no exception. Consider their horror, therefore, when we not only imported one right into the farm, but even wired off a portion of their orchard as Betsy's garden promenade. For the first day or two the four horses which we had there at the time showed the most intense agitation at this departure. They would not approach within some twenty yards of the wire fence, but spent their time high-tailing and high-stepping around the top of the paddock with indignant snorts. In the meantime Betsy took her pleasure undeterred, snuffling and wallowing along the side of the wire partition unconcernedly. By about the third day Quattuor was seen approaching the pig-run with ears pricked and head down. As soon as there was any sound or movement from the sow she would swing round and make away again, but within two further days all the horses were craning over the pig-run, straining to get a better view of the intruder. For about the next fortnight our routine was constantly disturbed by the necessity of having to disentangle horses from pig-wire. Betsy seemed to have a magnetic attraction for them which was quite irresistible. They could not leave her alone. They fought one another for the pleasure of rubbing their noses along her hairy back. They had to investigate every sample of her excreta and sniff every one of the innumerable holes she grubbed up. It was many weeks before the novelty apparently wore off and Betsy was once more allowed to take the air unaccompanied by her horsey retinue.

On thinking back over these instances, one factor seems to be common to them all—the overcoming of fear. A horse does not bother to investigate something of which it was not once very afraid and is not still half afraid. It is not curious about a thing unless it is in a state of uncertainty about it. It does not have to sniff at piles of gravel by the road when it knows that such piles do not hurt it. It does not have to investigate everything that a man has put down when it knows that the man is a friend. Curiosity, far from showing the complete absence of fear, indicates that fear is not very far away. The demonstration of curiosity, therefore, is an indication of a state of mind which should be treated with caution.

CHAPTER II

THE WORLD
AS THEY SEE IT

COLOUR

Some time ago a film was made about life in an American racing stable. The central and very attractive character was a race horse which, although infinitely faster and more valiant than any of its contemporaries, never won a race because it always jibbed at the starting gate and galloped away in the wrong direction! The reason, it transpired towards the end of the story, was that it had once been frightened by a woman in a red coat, which incident was always re-aroused in its mind whenever it saw the starter's red flag.

The plot of this story, however, is based on rather doubtful evidence. It is true that colours play a very important part in the lives of those creatures which can see them. But for a long time it has confidently been held that horses, like all mammals other than apes and monkeys, are colour blind.

There are two good reasons for such a belief. The first reason lies in the structure of their eyes. Although horses, like cows and other herbivorous animals are very active during the day time, their eyes closely resemble those of animals which live by night, and are adapted in a number of ways for seeing in the dark. Now most nocturnal animals, although they may see shapes, sizes and positions fairly accurately, have little need for colour-vision, and indeed show little evidence of having it. Hence, when one finds an animal with eyes built on the same principle as theirs, one tends to assume that this animal is colour-blind too.

The second reason for believing in the colour-blindness of horses lies in the colour of their coats. Unlike a number of birds and insects, the coats of horses occupy a range of sober browns. Even the highly attractive variations of the pie- and skewbald are striking not so much for their brilliance of hue as for their contrasts between light and darkness. Such variations as are to be found in the coat-colour of horses can easily be recognized by individuals who cannot recognize colours.

This last argument, however, is only corroborative, not conclusive. Man, like horses, it might be pointed out, does not grow hair in any of the pure primary colours, yet his powers of colour-vision are beyond dispute. In return it could be argued that man makes up for the parsimony of nature by adorning himself in the colours she has witheld and has thereby largely obviated the need for nature's covering at all. Were horses able to appreciate colours, they might fit themselves out in like manner, and the fact that they do not do so suggests that colours can mean little to them. However, these arguments are purely speculative, and examples can be taken from nature in favour of either conclusion.

Far more impressive evidence on the question of colour-vision in mammals comes from the various experiments which have been carried out on the subject. From the majority of these, the evidence still points to the failure of all mammals, other than apes and monkeys, to perceive colours. Contrary to popular belief, a rag of any colour, when waved, has the same effect on a bull as a red one. Moreover in none of the carefully controlled experiments carried out up till recent years have any mammals other than apes and monkeys shown a tendency to distinguish between colours except in a primitive and rudimentary way.

However, with the disturbing impact that increased knowledge usually has on one's most cherished beliefs, the whole question has lately been opened up again and has been thrown once more into confusion. In the first place, it seems that colour-vision may be possible in eyes of many different shapes and sorts, and that one can tell little about the ability and capacity of an eye from its external appearance. In the second place, one recent experimenter, Dr Grzimek, has published some work in which he claims to have been able to train horses to distinguish between colours. Two horses were used and each was led numerous times into a riding school in which were a number of mangers filled with oats. In front of one manger was hung a coloured card, and in front of the others were cards of various shades of grey. The horse was only allowed to eat from the manger containing the coloured card, and was held back whenever it tried to go to the others. Eventually when the horses were taken into the arena where the training had been carried out they would invariably make for the manger with the coloured card and would ignore the others. This indicates, according to Dr Grzimek, that colour-vision in these animals is *possible*, even if not very often utilized.[11]

Such experiments, however, are extremely hard to conduct, and it is difficult to be sure that the horses on this occasion were really responding to the colours as such and not to differences in light and shade, or even minute irregularities in the surface texture of the different cards of which the experimenter was himself unaware. Some years ago a somewhat similar argument raged around the question of whether bees could distinguish between colours. One experimenter, having noticed that bees in the fields tended to select flowers of certain colours, placed some yellow and blue pieces of paper on the ground in front of their hive, together with a variety of grey ones. He found that the bees almost invariably made for the coloured paper, leaving the grey pieces alone. This observer therefore not unnaturally argued that bees could distinguish colours, but at about the same time as these experiments were being carried out another man was investigating the same problem in a rather different way. He placed some bees in a dark room and confronted them with two lights of different colours and intensities. When the bees attempted to escape from the dark room they invariably made for the brighter of the two lights, regardless of its colour. This observer therefore concluded that bees are basically colour-blind and that when they select flowers or food trays they must really be responding to differences in shade.

The argument was not finally settled till it was discovered that both experimenters were partially right but that the true answer had escaped them both. Bees, like the majority of other animals, respond to different *aspects* of a stimulus in different situations. In the food seeking situation they respond to different colours more readily than to differences in brightness, but in the danger avoiding situation, such as when trying to escape from a dark room, they respond to different brightnesses more readily than to different colours.

The experiments leading to this realization not only solved a great argument but drew attention to a point most fundamental in the understanding of animal behaviour. It can be summed up as follows: *In a particular situation an animal will not respond to all the aspects of its environment which it has the sensory equipment to perceive. It will select as stimuli certain items only, and will behave as if unable to perceive others.* Thus, food seeking bees behave as if they could not distinguish between different intensities of light; danger avoiding bees behave as if they could not distinguish between colours. It therefore becomes necessary when trying to understand and analyse the senses of animals to analyse also the conditions in which the observations are carried out—i.e., to analyse the total situation. Moreover, even if it is known that an animal has the sensory equipment and ability to perceive certain aspects of its environment, it does not always follow that it will make use of the ability when it might be practicable and advantageous to do so. The important question with regard to colour-vision in horses, therefore, is not 'Can horses distinguish colours?', but 'Under what circumstances will horses distinguish colours?'

It is well known to anyone who has tried to jump in the Show ring that a horse faced for the first time with the highly coloured obstacles there will shy and goggle at them in terror. After his elimination for three refusals or for exceeding the time limit, the poor competitor will probably go home and erect in his own field a series of creations as like those in the ring as possible and will ride his horse round and over them until familiarity has bred contempt. If bars in his locality are

67

painted blue and yellow, he will have blue and yellow bars; if walls are red, he will put up red walls; and if he thinks he is ever likely to meet a green wall, he will have one that colour too.

But the building of show jumps is a very expensive and laborious business, and it would be a great help if we could be certain of the minimum number of different coloured obstacles it was necessary to provide in order to accustom our horses to all they were likely to meet outside. To do this, it might be as well to examine for a moment the very first assumption—namely that it is the *colour* of the jumps which frightens the horse and not some other feature of the total situation.

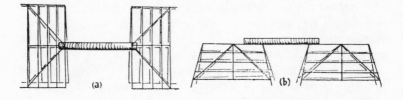

FIGURE 1

The same hurdles and bar, arranged differently, caused Nona great consternation, although the colour remained unchanged.

Because colours are so very striking to us, and because to us they do seem to be the most important feature of a show jump, it is very tempting to presume that it is the colours of which the horses are afraid. But horses will make an inordinate fuss about any strange object, regardless of its colour.

At the time I was first backing Nona, we were also schooling other more advanced ponies and horses for the local Shows. I had erected in one of the paddocks a series of obstacles mainly composed of white bars and hurdles. When the horses were not being schooled, they were turned out in this field, and Nona would browse around among the jumps, flicking them with her tail and prodding them with her nose.

68

One day, I decided to alter the course, and instead of standing the hurdles on end to form the wings, as in Fig. I(a), laid some of them down on their sides, as in Fig. I(b). As soon as Nona entered the field she stared, as if confronted by a ghost. It was many minutes before I could persuade her to get near enough to the obstacle to give it a smell, and even after this she remained suspicious of it for some time.

In this instance there could have been no question of unfamiliarity of colour. The hurdles were the same drab hurdles as Nona had been looking at for some weeks past; the bars were the same white bars. Her fear can only have been due to the change in their position and shape. A somewhat similar incident occurred some years later when I was schooling Gambit.

Gambit at that time was sharing a field with his father, Gamesman, who I was preparing for his first Show jumping venture. The only jump that I had to school over at that time was a homely affair composed of tin barrels which were stuck out in the field where the two horses were spending their evenings together. Both horses had been schooled to jump these barrels and did so without any fear. In order to make them more impressive and also to accustom Gamesman to the colour, I one evening took a bucket of whitewash up into the field and began to paint the barrels. Both horses were intrigued by my antics especially Gambit who did all he could to help or hinder my efforts by licking the wash off as fast as I put it on. Nevertheless, when, the next morning I saddled him and rode him up into the same field, he behaved as if he had never seen the barrels before. He would not go within twenty yards of them without snorting and shivering with fear, and it was not until I had laid them all down on their sides and made him walk along between them that he finally consented to jump over them. He had jumped them uncoloured without any trouble and he had seen them coloured. But to jump them coloured was something apparently, to him, quite new. From these experiences it seems possible to conclude that it is not only the colours which disturb inexperienced horses on the Show ground, but a sum total of the situation.

For my own part, I have never known a horse which was thoroughly used to jumping red walls shy at a green one, or vice versa. Nor have I ever known a horse which was schooled over black and white poles to jib at red and white ones, green and white ones, or blue and white ones. I *have* known horses that had only been schooled over red walls to stop in horror at cream or white ones, and vice versa, but here the differences in shade between darkness and brightness would be sufficient to account for the animal's anxiety.

Banks of flowers around obstacles, flags, and numbers are among other hazards whose upsetting influence is sometimes attributed to their colours. But the distractions caused by these may well be due to their minute movements, and movements, as will be mentioned later, are probably noticed by horses more readily and with greater suspicion than any other aspect of vision.

However, these considerations only indicate that the unhappiness of a novice horse when he sees a white jump for the first time may be explained on grounds other than his reactions to its colour. They do not prove that colours may not also play a part. What makes the matter even more complicated is the fact that some animals—and, indeed, people too—can see some colours although not others. Partially colour-blind human beings can distinguish blue and yellow just as well as other people, although both red and green look alike to them and resemble a dirty greyish brown. Some insects, such as bees, can see blue, yellow and violet just as we do, although, according to von Frisch, they are unable to see red.

Again, an object may appear one colour to us but quite a different colour to an animal or insect. Field poppies reflect light of two different sorts, one of which is visible to us but not to bees, and the other—at the ultra-violet end of the spectrum—which is visible to bees but not to us. The light we pick up gives us the impression of redness; what sort of impression the bees get from their ultra-violet rays it is impossible for us to imagine as our eyes simply do not register it.

Horses, like bees, may be able to perceive some colours in

the same way as we do, even if they cannot see them all. There is, in fact, no doubt that horses can see black and white, but these, it must be remembered, are not really colours. The impression of whiteness is due to the reflection on to the eyes of bright light; the perception of blackness is due to its absence. Perception of black and white depends on ability to distinguish intensities and shades, and not on the ability to see colours. Since black and white are so often regarded as colours, however, the reaction of horses to them may be considered here.

Horses are nearly always frightened at first by anything either very white or very black. Let us consider their fear of white objects first. It is sometimes suggested that the agitation shown by a horse at anything white is not so much due to fear as to excitement. Whiteness, as has just been said, is an impression gained from very strong illumination. When the eye sees an object as white it is receiving powerful stimulation, and is bombarding the brain with continuous messages. These messages will maintain the brain in a state of constant activity, and this may tire the animal or may at least make it uncomfortable. It is this discomfort rather than anything else which, according to some people, makes horses behave as they do. Certainly some species of animals do appear to suffer greatly if they are kept in very brightly lit surroundings. Orang-outangs, for instance, become quite hysterical, according to Hediger, if they are kept in brightly painted cages. Even light patches of colour on their walls are found to make them excited and agitated, but their behaviour quietens down as soon as the patches are darkened over.[15]

But what affects one animal may not affect others, and it does not follow from the example of a few other species that horses are affected by strong whites in this way. My own experiences, anyway, suggest that whiteness in itself is not unattractive to them. When I first went to Stones Farm there was no stabling there of any kind, so I had three new boxes built out of grey concrete blocks. After the three horses which I had there at the time had been thoroughly accustomed to all these boxes—being taken in each evening

71

and fed in each one in turn—I 'Snowcemed' the inside of the centre one white. In contrast to the others, the new interior decorations made it quite dazzling. The three horses were then taken individually up to the row of stables and allowed loose some distance from them, while we stood back and waited expectantly to see which box they chose to enter.

I must admit that, in view of the time and energy spent on our handiwork, they showed depressingly little reaction to it. If anything, there was a tendency to *prefer* the white box to the others, but this might have been accounted for either by curiosity or by the fact that the painted box was in the centre of the row and was therefore nearest to hand when the horses were loosed.

A second theory which has been put forward to explain a horse's fear of white objects is that of unfamiliarity. In the temperate zones of the earth inhabited by horses white objects appear rarely in nature. If an animal's coat is dead white, the animal is probably an albino, a freak of nature, and thus something to be avoided. But fear of whiteness may not necessarily be due to associations—even unconscious ones—such as this suggests. Professor Hebb made a very careful study of the things which provoked fear in a colony of apes he was once studying, and he noticed that it was neither the wholly unfamiliar nor the wholly familiar which frightened them so much as objects or events half-way between the two. A complete stranger entering the colony or a quite shapeless new toy might arouse curiosity but seldom aroused panic; whereas the sight of their keeper in unusual clothing or of a dummy ape with some of its limbs missing would readily put the whole colony into an uproar. It was the partial unfamiliarity of an object or incident, Hebb concluded, which really aroused fright—the eerie, not the unknown.[13]

A horse's fear of white objects can easily be understood on this basis. A familiar object painted white will be only half familiar and will hence become something ghost-like and uncanny. A small white object lying in the dark grass will present an island of strangeness in a familiar background. Hence, if a horse shies at a white object it is most important

72

that he should be allowed to have a good look at it—if possible a good sniff too—in order to assure himself that it is harmless.

A similar explanation cannot, however, account for a horse's fear of very dark objects and shadows. Although blackness has come to be regarded by man as symbolic of evil, and darkened places are taken to suggest the sinister, it is unlikely that animals have similar superstitions. On the other hand, the superstitions of man may themselves have a perfectly practical and physiological background. It will be remembered that the impression of blackness is due to the lack of light being reflected on to the eyes. Shadows, in the same way, are due to the absence of illumination. Hence, when faced with a black object one literally cannot see it as clearly as a white one, and when entering a dark room or a shadowy corner there is a well known danger of falling down unseen holes or walking into obscure snags.

This blindness does not usually last very long. The eye, by the process known as dark-adaptation, soon gets used to the situation, and after a little while a person may find himself able to see just as well in deep shadow as a few minutes before he was able to do in the sunlight. The process of dark-adaptation occurs in nearly all mammals. It is a purely physiological one and goes on without our being able to control it with the will. It occurs, moreover, at more or less the same rate in all the individuals of the same species, but this rate differs considerably between one species and another. In humans, the speed is comparatively fast. Within a few seconds of coming into a shaded room from the sun outside, the outline of large objects can usually be distinguished and the whole adaptive process is almost completed within twenty minutes. Curiously enough, those animals such as dogs and cats, whose eyes are made to enable them to see in the dark, take longer than us to adapt to sudden changes of illumination. Dogs, in whom the speed of dark-adaptation has been studied most carefully, seem to take nearly twice as long as man, so that if a man and his dog both enter a room at the same time the dog will still be able to see very little when the man is walking without difficulty.

73

Although the speed of dark-adaptation has never to my knowledge been studied in horses, it seems probable, since their eyes are also specialized for night vision, that the process is very slow in them as well. This would explain why, during the cross-country section of One-, Two-, and Three-Day Events, the fences most liable to upset horses are those which involve jumping out of sunlight into shadows or woods. To ask a horse to jump such a fence is like asking it to jump into the unknown, and no horse, unless in such a state of excitement that personal danger is forgotten, or unless so completely confident in its rider that it is prepared to do whatever is asked of it, will be at its best in such circumstances.

Slow and imperfect dark-adaptation might also account for the suspicion shown by many horses when asked to enter a strange stable or horse-box. On these occasions the smell of disliked predecessors may play a part (more of which will be discussed in Chapter III), but the dislike of stepping into the darkness is probably also an important factor. It may seem hard for an owner to believe that what appears to him as merely a dim shadow can possibly look like dense blackness to his horse, but such is possibly the case.

Horses which are difficult to load into strange boxes can often be persuaded to enter if they are allowed to stand for a few minutes on the ramp with their heads under cover. When their eyes have adapted to the change of brightness they will often prick their ears, put their noses down, and walk up voluntarily to examine the scene which has suddenly appeared in front of them. Attempts to force them up by running them to the ramp and hustling them from behind are, on the other hand, usually of little avail and only strengthen their suspicions.

An alternative way of overcoming the boxing difficulty is of course, to arrange the vehicle so that light falls on to the whole floor space. During the early post-war Occupation of Germany, one regiment kept several show jumpers which at first were transported to and from the shows in a very up-to-date horse-box. None of the horses had the slightest fear of travel or hesitated to enter the transport. After some

74

time the horse-box was replaced by a large, rough-hewn cattle-truck. This was completely enclosed, except for the usual slits near the roof. The horses refused to enter it, and for some time their reluctance was anthropomorphically attributed to snobbishness and dissatisfaction with the reduction of their circumstances. However, it occurred to the officer in charge that the darkness of the interior might play some part in the trouble. He insisted on having the roof stripped off the truck so that it was entirely open to the elements. Far from spurning their now even humbler conveyance, the horses walked into it without demur and travelled happily with their heads in the wind.

But although the eyes of horses and dogs may be slower to adapt to changes of illumination than those of man, they obviously get there in the end just as well as ours. Whether they get there better or not is difficult to say. Many stories have been told—some of which are quoted by G.L. Walls in his book on *The Vertebrate Eye*[39] —of night vision of horses, which suggest that they can see in the dim light very much better than us. I am myself not certain that this is so. At one time, my assistants and I spent a lot of time trying to find out what our horses did with themselves at night. More will be said of this later on. At the moment I would only like to point out that we ourselves managed to see a great deal in the darkness once our eyes had grown accustomed to it. It is true that we found we had to take very great precautions not to be spotted by our 'prey' and during our manoeuvres on the first nights we would frequently find ourselves outwitted by them. After a lengthy stalk on hands and knees, we would peer over a stable door to find a beady eye fixed on us with unfeigned curiosity; after an agonizing crawl along the side of a prickly hedge, we would look up to find the horses we were tracking in full flight at the opposite end of the field. We soon realized that in order to observe the animals at rest without disturbing them, it was necessary to take all the precautions normally employed when hunting wild animals. Camouflage was the first essential. A fawn mackintosh or a duffle coat would stand out 100 yards away and cause immediate panic. It was only when wearing dark clothes and black scarves over our faces that we managed to get within reasonable distance of them unobserved.

But the thing that struck us most was their fear at being approached like this in the dark—a fear which suggests that although they could see a certain amount, they did not see well enough to recognize us.

On another occasion I was trying to show off a pony to some prospective buyers who did not unfortunately arrive to see it till almost dark. They were very keen to see the pony jump, and it was in fact a bold and willing jumper. This particular evening, however, it approached every fence in the half-light slowly and cautiously, stopping to have a good look at each before jumping, as if uncertain where or what each obstacle was. It seems probable, therefore, that horses do not really see very much better at night than a well dark-adapted human, to whom paths, trees, and gates may be recognizable even though their exact shapes and positions are difficult to define.

Before leaving the subject of colours, it might be mentioned that although there is no direct evidence that horses can *see* colours in the same way as we do, this does not prove that they are unable to feel them in some other manner. Chickens ignore colours most of the time, and, like mammals, behave as if they too were colour-blind. Yet it has been found that they will feed more voraciously and happily if surrounded by the so-called 'warm' colours (red and yellow) than by the so-called 'cold' ones (blue and violet). This, and the very fact that we do often refer to colours in terms of warmth, softness, hardness, coldness, etc., indicates that colours not only affect the eyes but may also be perceived by other senses. But such perception is very different from the experience gained by vision and must therefore be left to another section of this book.

PERCEPTION OF SHAPE AND SIZE

At first consideration it might be taken for granted that if an animal can see at all it will see differences of shape and size in the same way as we do. These perceptions, moreover, seem to be automatic and innate. We do not have to think in

76

order to tell a circle from a square or a triangle from an oblong. Nor do we have to learn anything in order to tell which is the larger of two objects such as a hen's egg and a football. We tend to take it for granted that differences such as these will be recognized automatically by any creature with eyes. Colour-blindness is understandable, but nobody could fail to see a gap in a fence if one was there, nor, unless he were mad, would he appear to see a gap if none existed. Yet on occasions some animals, especially horses, *will* behave as if they saw non-existent obstacles in their paths or as if they completely failed to recognize their friends.

One day I happened to be carrying a pair of hurdles across a field beside the paddock in which my horses were turned out. The horses had seen me every day for many months and they had, moreover, been schooled regularly over the hurdles I was carrying. Yet as I approached them now they lifted their heads and stood quite rigid, snorting in fear and apprehension. Then off they went a few paces at a gallop, stopping abruptly after a little to turn round and have another stare. Even when I approached them later without the hurdles to pacify them, they treated me at first with the greatest suspicion and were not happy till they had given both me and the hurdles a few satisfactory sniffs.

On other occasions horses will fail to recognize their own companions if the latter have been clipped, are saddled differently, or are turned out in rugs, and will savage them or kick them as they would do strangers. When I first observed this, I was inclined to believe that the unrugged horse was jealous of its pampered companion and was taking it out of him in this way, but after watching one incident I came to the conclusion that the aggression was really a symptom of fear and due to the tendency, common alike in man and animals, of wanting to hit before being hit oneself. Unus was very thin-skinned, and in the winter I had to keep him in a New Zealand rug when he was out at grass. One evening in September, about two months after the brown pony, Septem, had joined the establishment, I decided that the weather was cold enough for Unus to start wearing his rug. He was brought in for his evening feed, as usual, and the rug was put on him before he was turned out again. When he went back into the field with the others, Septem, who was standing a little way from the gate, threw up his head and gave a significant snort of fear. As Unus began to walk over towards the other horses, Septem turned tail and fled a few paces. When Unus began to graze, Septem returned and trotted round him inquisitively, stopping every now and then about ten yards from him to have another look. Each time Unus moved, or if, when swishing his tail, he beat it against the tarpaulin with a clatter, Septem would leap around and rush a few paces further away. Gradually he approached within striking distance, and then, with a wild burst of courage, laid back his ears and went for poor Unus with bared teeth. The old horse merely hopped off a few paces and went on eating, whereupon, Septem's courage increasing, he returned to the attack. It was a long time before, realizing apparently that the apparition was harmless, Septem approached with enough composure to have a good smell at the rug and satisfy himself that it only covered an old friend.

It is not only changes to individual objects themselves which may provoke fear. The situation in which the object is placed has a vital role. When studying the hand reared orphaned foals at my veterinary neighbour's establishment I thought it would be interesting to see how they responded to horse models, both whole and mutilated. While 'normal' horses respond to horse models and to their own reflections in a mirror as they would to other horses, I thought it was quite possible that foals which had been reared in social isolation would fail to do so. An artistic friend of mine was therefore commissioned to make two dummy horses, one of which was painted a uniform beige (or bay) while the other was painted in broad beige and white diagonal stripes. My argument ran that if the shape was recognized by the foals as being that of a member of its own species the striped model would arouse fear, whereas if it were not so recognized it would only arouse interest.

Before showing the models to the subjects in the intended experiment, I decided it would be as well to try them on my own 'families' first, and therefore took them up to erect them in the field where the mares and foals were spending their Summer. Before I had even reached the gate, however, the mares started snorting with horror and indignation and herded their offspring well away to the farthest corner of the terrain. Nor did they approach within 100 yards of the area where I had been till I and both models had been removed for some time. Later that day it happened that one of the mares had to be brought into the yard where I had left the two models on my return from the pilot experiment, and to my amazement she walked quietly past them with little more than a casual glance. Actually, inside a loose-box the models seemed to be even less fear provoking. There they were sniffed over quietly—and even chewed. That the lack of anxiety aroused by the stimuli was due to the different environment rather than to familiarity was shown by the fact that back in her own field, the mare showed just as great a panic as she had on the first occasion.

Perception of shape and size has been one of the most intensively studied branches of psychology, and although there is still much to be learned about them a great deal has already been found out. In the first place, it is now generally accepted that, contrary perhaps to expectation, the ability to distinguish shapes and sizes is *not* a fixed, inborn ability but is continually changing with practice and experience. In the second place, the things that a person is conscious of seeing at any given time depend on a delicate co-ordination between the information supplied by his eyes and various other activities that are going on in his mind at the same time, such as voluntary movements, emotional tensions, desires, and expectations. We tend to pick out and see in our whole environment only certain selected items, concentrating our attention on these and ignoring others. The classical example is that of a golfer who, when looking for a lost ball, becomes aware of innumerable small white objects dotted about the fairway which, if his mind had been occupied with other concerns, he would never have seen.

In the third place, preoccupation plays a part in determining not only *what* one sees but also *how* one sees things. This has been demonstrated in innumerable psychological experiments. To quote just one example, an ambiguously shaped figure which could have been taken to represent either a coffee-pot or a windmill was shown to two groups of people. By prearranged conversation the first group had been made to think of a coffee-pot and the second to think of a windmill. When the people in the two groups were asked what the ambiguous figure looked like to them, those in the first group naturally said it looked like a coffee-pot; those in the second that it resembled a windmill.

Preoccupation not only directs our attention: it may even encourage us to think we have seen things which are not there. A misprint in a fairly straightforward line is notoriously difficult to spot, just as is a missing piece in an otherwise completed object. In the same way, unfamiliar objects may be regarded as quite familiar if they are seen in a familiar setting, and familiar ones strange if met out of their usual context. The face behind the counter is easily recognized in its appropriate shop; but if it suddenly confronts us on the station platform or in the middle of the street we may have great difficulty in placing the owner.

A further important aspect of visual perception is the influence on it not only of immediate experiences but also of those things which happened long ago. We know from photographs and from the laws of optics that, as objects recede into the distance, their visual size diminishes—that is to say, the image they reflect on to the eye gets smaller. Yet our minds and eyes have learned to make allowances for this. Automatically, and without any effort, they perform immense feats of adjustment, so that a six-foot man still looks six feet tall, whether he is seen two yards or twenty yards away. Again, we know from various measuring instruments that a piece of white paper, if it is lying in shadow, will only reflect grey light on to the eyes. Yet, because we *know* it to be white, our eyes make allowances for its perceived colour and still *see* it as white. We know now that such an ability is due to past experiences and is not inborn, because it was discovered by von Sendern that people who were born blind, due to congenital cataracts, and whose sight was given to them after they had reached maturity, are not able to see things in the same way as others until they have had a good deal of practice. These people have to learn to see much as we have to learn to read. It is apparently only because we learned to recognize shapes and sizes at such an early age that they seem so obvious later on. By using the term 'learning' here, I do not mean to imply that conscious effort is involved. The eyes seem to develop the ability to make these adjustments of their own accord if they are given sufficient

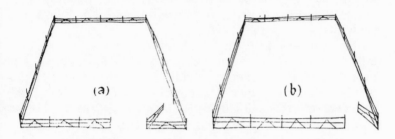

FIGURE 2
A flock of sheep refused to enter the pen when the gap was placed in one side (a), but entered willingly through a gap in the corner (b).

practice when young, and the brain develops the ability to interpret the messages in the same way.

From experiments it appears that in most animals visual sensations are reconstructed in much the same way as ours. In the first place, animals, like us, tend to see the things which they expect to see and fail to see those they do not. If an object is complete except for a small gap, the gap is often overlooked. In our own case gaps have to be fairly small before we are likely to overlook them, but in the case of some animals this is not so. In a flock of sheep I once found this gap to be the size of a hurdle! I was trying to drive the small flock into a pen and had left an opening for them in one side, as shown in Fig. 2(a). I drove the sheep up to this gap on innumerable occasions and from every possible angle, but, although eager to enter the pen, they seemed utterly incapable of realizing that they were able to do so.

They would charge up to the edge of the gap, then hesitate at one side, look into it, and shoot past it as if terrified they might be tempted to try to go through. After some hours of gradually accumulating heat and anger, I decided to see what would happen if I altered the position of the gap and placed it on one corner, as in Fig. 2(b). The hurdles bounding the gap were now no longer part of one thing—one side—but belonged to different entities altogether. There was, in fact, no gap, merely a space between two sides. At the very first attempt the sheep now ran along one side and turned into the pen without hesitation.

Although horses may not be quite as blind as sheep in this respect, young horses are often equally reluctant to go through narrow spaces in the middle of a hedge or ditch. Like the sheep, they will treat the apparition of a space with great suspicion, snorting and goggling as if convinced there must be something wrong; and often, when finally persuaded to advance, they will do so with a leap, as if they really saw some form of barricade. Perhaps, after all, they did. Eyes, even our own, are extremely good at fabricating false evidence and, as at the cinema, will tell their owners very convincingly that something is going on—in this case movement on the screen ahead—when the intellect knows that it is not.

Animals, like men, may also fail to recognize a familiar object if its setting is slightly altered. I have already quoted several instances of this. There was the time I was crossing the horses' field carrying some hurdles; there was the time I laid some hurdles on their sides instead of upright and wanted Nona to walk round them; there was the time Septem first saw Unus in his New Zealand rug. These examples may be criticized because something had been slightly altered in the object itself as well as in the settings, but it is not difficult to find instances in which the object remains the same and the alteration lies only in the circumstances surrounding it.

In the previous chapter I described how the horror shown by the horses at the arrival of Betsy, the pig, gradually gave way to fascination, and how jealousy and social prestige became involved in scuffles for the privilege of sniffing at the sow's back. Quinque, the three-year-old pony whom I had been breaking-in at the time, had been joining in this pursuit as whole-heartedly as any of the others, when one day I decided to exercise her around the field alongside Betsy's run. The pony was in a skittish mood that morning and obviously on the alert for an excuse to show fight. She found it in Betsy. Some forty yards from the wire fence over which she had been straining only a few minutes before she went quite rigid with fear, and it was with the greatest difficulty that I got her to approach it at all. Each time Betsy squealed or grunted an invitation, Quinque jumped back as if struck, in exactly the same way as she had done on the first day of Betsy's arrival. It was not until she had finally been urged right up to Betsy and persuaded to smell her that she finally calmed down. It seemed as though, when saddled and bridled, Quinque saw her environment in quite a different light, just as Gambit did when ridden up to the white barrels for the first time. The familiar brown spotted back became something new, and evoked the same reaction that the sight of a new pig would have done.

The same sort of behaviour can frequently be seen in horses introduced for the first time to the horrors and distractions of a busy Show ground. If led quietly past tents, bands, flags, and merry-go-rounds, they may appear to lose their fear quickly, but as soon as they are mounted and ridden up to the same diversions their original apprehension provisionally returns.

However, familiarity not only breeds contempt; it can also bring judgement. If a man sees enough objects of the same sort, he learns not only to recognize them as a group or class but also to recognize small differences between the different individuals. To the huntsman one hound becomes quite different from another, and even sheep develop an individuality to the shepherd. But of just as much practical importance as this is the development, through familiarity and experience, of the recognition of likenesses—'connoisseurship'. A person who has seen a lot of dogs will finally recognize as dogs, even those of unique parentage. A person who is

83

familiar with Ming vases will recognize one of this dynasty when he sees it, no matter what the setting.

It is possible that some animals—horses among them—do not form these 'generalizations' as quickly as Man, and that this is one of the reasons some people regard them as unintelligent; but as most trainers are well aware, they can be formed eventually. The more experience gained by a horse of jumping different obstacles, the more easily it will recognize among what it sees those things which are intended to be jumped; the more it sees of different kinds of traffic, the sooner it will learn that traffic does it no harm.

One point of particular interest is how horses recognize by sight members of their own species. When describing the experiment with the striped model, I mentioned that 'normal' horses recognize themselves in mirrors and recognize horse models as being of their own species. I have also referred to the fact that animals raised by foster parents of a different species may fail to do this. But how do animals learn what they are? In nearly all species this takes place at a very early age and is due to the activity of the mother. Foals, like lambs, are born with a tendency to follow any moving object and therefore 'heel' to their dams as soon as they can walk. (Not all species do this. In goats, the young tend to 'freeze' as soon as the dam moves off). When the foal is due, the dam therefore goes off by herself to some spot behind a bush or tree or mound, and drops the foal in private. For the next few days she takes great pains to ensure that she and only she is the moving object it sees, by continually placing herself between her foal and other horses when they are present. I was able to observe the way in which they do this by an example of Nauri with her first foal Nymphette.

Nauri, Nuki's eldest daughter, caught me out by producing Nymphette a week before she was due and before she had been removed from the field in which she had been running out with other horses. Although when they were discovered, the mare and foal were still by themselves and were quickly removed to a separate paddock adjoining the big field which at that time was occupied by a two-year-old, Gracie, and a yearling, Navy Blue. These two youngsters, who had been left

84

behind were furiously jealous of the new arrival who they didn't feel they had had a chance to examine closely the night before. Soon they were galloping up and down the fence between the two fields or leaning over it as far as their necks would reach. Finally, Navy Blue was aroused to unbearable excitement and jumped the fence. Then the fun began. Each time Navy Blue approached within yards of mother and child, Nauri would lay back her ears and dive towards him, then swing around to kick. Navy Blue would dance out of range but meanwhile the foal, which had begun to follow Nauri in one direction, would continue in that direction following the moving object, which by then happened to be Navy Blue. Then Nauri would set out in pursuit of the pair of them, dive between yearling and foal again and push the foal out to one side.

The other visual and social experiences a foal has at this time may also affect its behaviour later on. If a foal is exposed to the presence of humans during its first few hours of life, Waring found it tends to show considerably less fear of Man later on.[41] This is not to say that it is necessarily more tractable when it comes to be handled (having less fear can actually make it more resistant) but it is less apprehensive of the human presence. Such foals also tend to show greater independence in that they tend to graze further from their dams in the paddock. Waring found that the effect of early visual experience depended on the length of time it lasted as well as on its nature. A passive human figure (in fact a lifeless model) had less effect than an active one, while this was in turn less effective than a person who actually played with, and responded to, the foal's advances. My own experience with different foals, however, makes me wonder how much later behaviour is due to early experience and how much to the individual itself. My first breeding mare, Nuki, had her first three offspring in the field at home. Nauri, the first, arrived in the pitch dark at 11.30 p.m., and no one was able to go near her until the next morning. As soon as I approached the mare and foal, however, Nuki pushed Nauri up to be admired, and the little creature did not hesitate to sniff me over from head to feet. The second one, Gamesman, arrived at 8.30 a.m. I was with him for about ten minutes immediately during and after his birth, but did not go near him again till about seven hours later. When I did so, he, like Nauri, was only too anxious to examine me and be examined. Nuki's third son, His Nibs, was also born outside but at 4.30 p.m., and was not approached till the following morning. He also was friendly enough, as was Nuki's fourth foal, Nuit, and her sixth, Noisette. However, her fifth foal, Top Notch, and her seventh, Navy Blue, were quite different. All were by thoroughbred horses; all were foaled at home and all were produced by Nuki so quickly and easily and with so little warning that Gamesman's birth is the only one which I actually witnessed. Top Notch did not appear to be any different from the others, yet he was six weeks old before anyone was able to lay so much as a finger on him. One could not really even see him clearly until then, for the moment a person approached he would rush away behind his mother and stand firmly with his back to the visitors. Navy Blue's reaction was somewhat different. From the moment he was born he took the line 'You're not going to get the better of me'. Although he would often approach and try to investigate a human being, as soon as the human put a hand out to touch him he would turn round and make off.

After this, Nuki had three more foals all by the same sire, Abyss. The first one, a colt, Nubian, was bold and fearless from the moment he was born; so was the next one, a filly, Niobe. The third, however, another filly, Nebula, took after Navy Blue and did not want to have anything to do with Man.

The offspring of Nuki's son, Gamesman, are just as varied in their behaviour. Moreover, the extent to which immediate reactions persist or alter seems difficult to predict. The fearless Nauri, went off with her dam to stud when she was eight days old and on her return six weeks later would not come near me or allow herself to be touched. Instead of coming forward to sniff and lick me as she had done before her departure, she kept as far away as possible. Not until after I had forced her to submit to being handled (in order to tend a wound on one of her legs) did she get over this phase—but once she had been handled again, all her old friendliness reasserted itself. Top Notch responded to his very first contact with Man (at the age of ten weeks) by losing all his fear at once and becoming thereafter almost too friendly. Not only would he immediately come up to any visitor in the field, but he would plant himself firmly between the visitor and the gate so that the visitor could not leave again without pushing him aside—a contact which he loved and sought to prolong by pushing back. Nebula was not forced in any way, but by degrees she herself began to approach me, and once we had made contact she became almost as demanding of attention as Top Notch. Different, however, was Nymphette, Nauri's first daughter. For the first four months of her existence she would come up to within a few inches of any human who approached her, take a sniff, and then lay back her ears and curl her lips in a snarl as if the smell was just too repulsive, turning round at the same time and hunching her quarters as if threatening to kick. When she was finally caught and forced to submit to handling, her resentment continued. Unlike Top Notch or Nebula who were both easy to catch as soon as they discovered they were not going to be hurt, Nymphette remained apprehensive and defensive for weeks, snarling, grinding her teeth and prepared to kick out at the first opportunity. Not until I decided she had had enough man-handling for the time being and could be left alone, did she drop her resentment and actually approach to be stroked. Then, as if to make up for the weeks of petting she had missed, she also started demanding extra attention and extra fuss.

MOVEMENT AND POSITION

Although some horses will shy at a very near object, as if failing to see it properly, the same animals will often notice movements several miles away which are scarcely discernible to man. When I was still at school, the hounds used to meet quite near my home on two days a week, and as my lessons finished at mid-day I used to rush home on these occasions, get on to my pony, and by about 1 p.m. I would be scouring the countryside to pick up the hunt. Often I would be riding

87

along, with my own eyes skinned but unable to see anything, when my pony would suddenly prick his ears, lift up his head, and stare in a certain direction. Usually by concentrating hard on the way he indicated, I could finally make out what he was seeing, but even when I could not do so I found that by trusting to his perspicacity and by riding in whichever direction he indicated, I was never very wrong.

The difference between a horse's ability to see static objects close at hand and moving ones far away can be accounted for by several factors. In the first place, the eyes of almost all animals, including man, can pick up a moving object more readily than a stationary one, not only in the far distance but also at comparatively close range. A person who cannot see a stationary object 1 in. in diameter two yards from him will be able to see one half that size as soon as it moves. An animal which is almost invisible to its predator while 'frozen' becomes quite obvious as soon as it moves.

The ability of horses to perceive slight movement, however, is quite outstanding and was illustrated in a famous case at the beginning of this century. A German of considerable repute, Herr von Osten, claimed to have trained a horse to answer questions, tell the time, be capable of four different methods of arithmetical calculation, and many other feats suggesting that it had powers of reasoning and abstraction little inferior to those of man. The problems could be given either verbally or in writing, and Clever Hans, as the stallion was called, would tap out his replies on a board at his feet, using one fore-leg to denote the tens and the other to denote the digits.[19]

Herr von Osten's claims and the behaviour of Clever Hans aroused such interest and raised so many points of philosophical interest, that a committee of eminent scientists was set up to investigate the matter. They were given every support and cooperation by von Osten himself and concluded that there was no trickery or fraud. However, shortly after this a private investigator exploded the secret. He asked the horse questions whose nature was unknown to the men present, so that no one but himself knew the answers to them, and he noticed that under these conditions the horse was powerless to do even the simplest sums or solve the most elementary problems. Indeed, Hans gave the impression of being far more interested in the questioners than in the question. The investigator therefore turned his attention away from the horse and on to the behaviour of the people in charge of him. Close scrutiny finally revealed the fact that the humans were making slight, almost imperceptible and completely unconscious movements with their heads or bodies each time the horse was due to stop tapping, and it

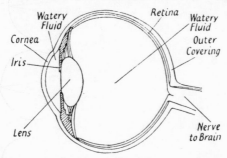

FIGURE 3
Diagram showing a section through the eye of a mammal.

became clear that the horse had learned to pick up and interpret these movements rather than work out the problems for himself.

But although the horse's eye is like those of other animals in being very perceptive to movement, it differs from a great many in having a clumsy method of focussing. As is well known our eyes cannot keep things of different distances all in focus at the same time. When an object in the far distance is seen clearly, those closer to hand will appear blurred: when a near object is in focus, the more distant ones are blurred. Yet a normal young person can switch over from near to distant with comparatively little difficulty.

To understand how this comes about, it is necessary to consider the structure of the eye itself. The eyes of most mammals consist of two cavities, each filled with a transparent fluid (Fig. 3). They are divided from one another by a layer of opaque, elastic tissue, the iris, in the centre of which is the transparent lens. Light from objects outside passes through these cavities and through the lens, and finally reaches a layer of cells at the back of the eye, the retina, which is connected by a bundle of nerves to the brain. As light reaches these cells, it sets off electrical and chemical

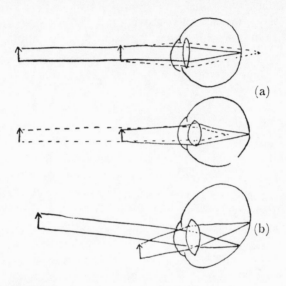

FIGURE 4
Focusing mechanism of the eye: (a) The method used in the human eye–lens accommodation. (b) The method used in the horse–the ramp-retina.

processes in them, which activate the nerves to send a message to the brain.

Now in order that the rays of light from an object may be bent and brought to form an image exactly on the retina–neither in front of it nor behind it–the lens makes itself round and fat or flat and thin according to the distance of the object from the eye (Fig. 4[a]). This is known as accommodation. As a person gets older and the elasticity of the lens decreases, this often becomes more difficult and he has to have extra lenses fittes to glasses in front of his eyes to help.

But the lens inside a horse's eye has no elasticity or powers of accommodation, and can only bend rays of light from all objects the same amount. It gets over the difficulty of focusing by having the retina arranged on a slope or ramp, so that the bottom part is much nearer the lens than the top part (Fig. 4[b]). In order to focus on objects at different distances it has to raise or lower its head so that the image is brought into contact with that part of the retina the right distance away. For a horse living in the wild state, this is an extremely practical arrangement, for while its head is down feeding both near objects at its feet and those in the distance above the horizon will all be in focus at the same time; but for horses that are being ridden and driven it is not so good, for it means that the horse is always having to alter the position of its head in order to focus on different objects. When it is made to hold its head up, near objects at its feet will always be out of focus and will only be seen imperfectly. This is probably why horses often shy at close objects, and why, when they are being ridden over rough country or jumps, they should be encouraged to keep their heads low.

The difficulty horses have in focusing must make it very hard for them to judge distances accurately. This difficulty is probably not helped by the way their eyes are set on their heads. There are many ways in which we can judge depth and distance, but one of the cues on which we rely most strongly is binocular vision—that is, the ability to see a thing with both eyes simultaneously. In order to have binocular vision, both eyes must be situated close together on one side of the head, and they must be able to take in very much the same scene. Since each eye takes in the scene from a slightly different angle, however, it will receive a slightly different image. The images received by the two eyes are superimposed inside the brain, and the combined result—three-dimensional vision—causes objects not only to gain the appearance of solidity but also to 'stand out' in space.

The difference which such an arrangement makes to the perception of distance can easily be discovered by a little experiment which anyone can carry out on himself. While sitting at the dining- or writing-table, close one eye and then move the forefinger directly away from the body until it is judged as being exactly over a chosen object, say the salt-cellar or an ink-bottle. Having reached the spot which the experimenter believes to be over his target, let him open his other eye and he will almost certainly be amazed at his error.

The ability to judge distances is very important to animals of prey, and it is probably for this reason that such species usually have their eyes set together in front of their heads. But horses, for whose survival a wide field of vision is the more important, have their eyes set one on either side so that each takes in a very wide but largely different scene. When the images of the two eyes are superimposed, the result is not one small three-dimensional field as is the case with us but a large, predominantly flat panorama. They do indeed have a small three-dimensional area of vision, but it is not nearly so large as ours, and it is not certain whether they use it very much.

In order to see what life would be like without binocular vision, my assistants and I once spent some time at Stones Farm going about our daily routine with one eye closed! Not only did we carry out our usual chores in this way, but we also tried jumping small obstacles (on foot), and I even (probably to the danger of both the public and myself) drove the car a distance of 12 miles into Oxford and back, closing first one eye and then the other.

From our experiences we all came to very much the same conclusions. The far distance and very close objects looked much as they had always done; it was predominantly at the middle-distance that difficulties arose. In the beginning we found serious difficulty in judging the speed with which we were approaching obstacles. At one moment things would seem to be very far away (to belong to the far distance) and at the very next they would suddenly seem to be on top of us. We tended to find ourselves right underneath a jump before being ready to take off, and when driving the car I kept finding myself having to brake suddenly in order to avoid running into the backs of vehicles which a moment before had seemed a long way off. From such experiences it was easy to appreciate why horses, who probably have little use for binocular vision in their free state, have difficulty in judging distances. Unless it is told when to take off for a fence, a young horse almost always tends to get too close to it, and most horses are invariably happier jumping perpendicular obstacles than those lying horizontally. However with practice we began to find ourselves overcoming the difficulties of monocular vision. We did so by giving up our dependence on direct perception of depth and by making allowances for the faulty information of our eyes. We began looking for different sorts of clues to tell us how far away different things were, and we found that different cues were available when one really needs them.

The tendency to make allowances like this was scarcely conscious or intentional. Our eyes and brains seemed to make the necessary adjustments of their own accord, and our muscles obeyed the new signals automatically. The speed and completeness with which such adaptations can be made are very remarkable, and although our own case was not very impressive, an experiment carried out by psychologists some years ago demonstrates the amazing powers of adaptation of which the body is capable.[23] They were started by Dr. Stratton, who wondered how long it would take him to get used to living in a world in which everything was seen upside down. He made a pair of spectacles in which the lenses reversed every image that reached his eyes, and he wore these for some months all the time he had his eyes open. After a time he found that he was able to move about in this topsy-turvy world as freely and easily as before—in fact, things no longer looked upside down at all. As soon as this stage was reached he took off his lenses; now the world seemed upside down to him once more, and it took him some time to re-accustom himself to its normal appearance. Other investigators repeated Stratton's experiment, but put on and took off the reversing lenses every time they had adapted themselves to the altered appearance of the world. They noticed that each time they changed over, the adaptation to the altered cues occurred more quickly, until a time was finally reached when the world seemed the same way up to them whether in fact they were wearing the reversing lenses or not.

Adaptation of this sort, which depends on neither conscious effort nor intelligence, is probably as frequent in all ranks of the animal world as it is in man, and horses given sufficient practice and opportunity nearly always learn to judge their distances from jumps accurately. But practice and experience are essential to this type of learning, which cannot be unduly hurried.

CHAPTER III

HOW HORSES FEEL

HOMING EXPERIMENTS

Although horse-drawn transport is slow and laborious
compared to modern methods of travel, it has one great asset
which can never be achieved by motors and aeroplanes. The
traveller seldom needs a map in order to get home. Be he five
or fifteen miles away, in familiar territory or new, he has
only to throw his reins on his horse's neck for his beast to
convey him back—if not to his own door, at least to that of
the animal's stables.

To what exactly this 'homing' behaviour is due is one of
the great mysteries of nature. For a long time man searched
in vain for a special sense organ in those animals capable of
homing, believing that they must possess the ability to sense
things such as the magnetism of the earth's electrical forces.
However, most of the experiments and observations carried
out recently seem to indicate that the mystery is less
profound, even if no less exciting. Different species of
animals seem to find their way around and achieve their
orientation in space by highly specialized but different
aspects of those sense organs familiar to all, and do not
possess any extra special powers. Bees, for instance, are
guided by visual landmarks and by their susceptibility to the
polarization of the sun's light; in dogs and cats, homing is
believed to depend on a very acute sense of smell.[33] Hence, a
careful study of the homing behaviour in particular species,
although it may not tell us very much about this function in
particular, may all the same give us some very valuable

95

information about the animals' sensitivity.

It was, at any rate, in the hope that this might be so that I myself began to make a systematic and experimental study of the homing behaviour of horses.

The first experiment was made with Unus and Peter. I loaded these two, together with one of my assistants, Sally, into the trailer (the windows of which had been covered up) and transported them on to the downs about twenty miles from home. We unloaded in country which I knew that none of them had ever seen before and set off at a hunting canter for about two miles in a semi-circle, finishing at a point some distance beyond the trailer and away from home. There I asked Sally to tell me in which direction she herself would go. She admitted that, after leaving home, she knew we had started off along a certain road because at one point I slowed down and sounded the horn as I always did when going over a particularly dangerous bridge. However, after that she had no idea of the route we had taken, nor of the direction of home. She had a good idea where to find the trailer because she realized that we had ridden in a semi-circle since leaving it, but that was all.

After giving the horses a short breather, we dropped the reins and relaxed our legs so as not to give them any aids, and then urged them forwards at a walk, allowing them to go in whatever direction they liked. The only times they were checked or guided were in order to prevent them crossing sown fields or entering private property. They set off at once in the direction of home and trailer, without making any attempt to retrace the route taken by the 'hunt' and without any apparent doubts as to the direction they wanted to take. Resolutely and firmly they kept on their course, even though in so doing they occasionally came up against fences or entered blind alleys from which they had to retreat.

The second experiment was performed with Sally, Unus and Peter again, but on a different part of the downs. After unloading, we rode a 'hunt' this time in a figure of eight (Fig. 5), ending up once more on the far side both of home and trailer. As soon as they were released the horses once again made for the trailer, but this time we decided to see what they would do after arriving there. Instead of stopping and dismounting, as we had done before, we remained immobile in the saddle. The result was rather surprising. As we came level with the trailer, Unus pricked his ears, tossed his old head, and suddenly broke into a canter, setting off for

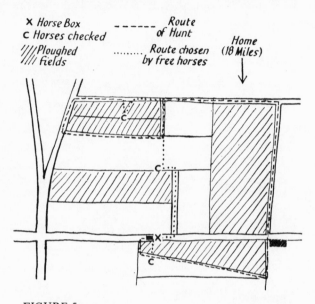

FIGURE 5

Route taken during the 'homing' experiment in which the original 'hunt' was ridden in a figure of eight. The horses did not attempt to retrace their steps when freed, but set off at once for home, without even stopping at the trailer.

home some twenty miles away. Instead of being drawn towards the trailer, as I had imagined he would, it seemed now as though he had really been aiming for something far more distant, (yet far more important to him)—his own stable.

I decided to check this conclusion by another experiment. This time I loaded Unus and the brown Fell pony, Billy Bunter, into the trailer, together with a different assistant,

97

Mary, and transported them on to a new part of the downs. I arranged our 'hunt' this time in a semi-circle, to end up almost directly between the trailer (about one mile away) and home (some fourteen miles away), so that if the horses made for one they would have to make away from the other. The course they chose is shown in Fig. 6. There was never the

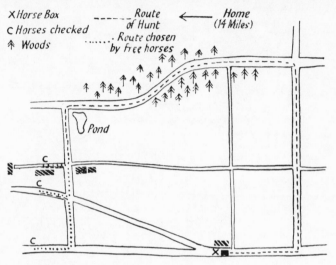

FIGURE 6
Map showing the route taken during the 'homing' experiment in which the horses were stopped and freed between the trailer and home. They consistently chose the home direction in preference to that of the trailer.

slightest doubt about the way they wanted to go: they resolutely turned their backs on the trailer and made in the direction of the stables. After some distance, we checked them and made them walk back some way towards the trailer. When released a second time they behaved in exactly the same way. Without hesitation, both turned straight for home—in fact, we had quite a struggle to get them back to the trailer at all. Every little lane, gateway or path we passed acted as a magnet to the reluctant beasts, who would swoop

98

off down it while they thought our attention was distracted.

How the horses gained their knowledge of the whereabouts of home, however, was a mystery. From the way in which the experiments had been arranged it was almost impossible that they could have relied on vision, but this conclusion was further corroborated by their behaviour during the tests. If firmly determined to go northwards, they would turn down any lane, drive or path leading in that direction, even though it might be quite obvious that the lane led to a dead-end and that their steps would have to be retraced. It was not until they actively came up against an obstacle that they would appear to be aware of its presence and adopt means of circumventing it.

With vision ruled out, I began to think of other senses which might have been used, especially smell. That scent plays an important role in territorial recognition in most species is well established. Salmon appear to find their way back into the rivers and streams in which they were spawned by means of this, being sensitive to concentrations of as little as 3×10^{-18} (representing the dilution of one thimbleful of liquid in 'a body of water sixty times the size of Lake Constance')—according to Ricard.[33]

The favourite method for examining dependence on a certain sense organ—namely cutting it out and seeing how the animals behaves without it—was not one which I was prepared to employ on any of my horses, let alone my best hunter, but fortunately there are other, even if more equivocal, methods of examining dependence on smell.

As everyone knows, scent is carried on the wind. A source down-wind of an animal may pass quite close to it unheeded, while one up-wind, even if some miles away, will create quite a stir. Unfortunately, no note had been made, at the time of the previous experiments, of the direction of the wind on those occasions, so that a new series of experiments had to be conducted, specifically to examine this point. Two of the experiments were carried out to the north of the stables and two to the south of them. During one experiment in each direction the wind was blowing strongly towards the stable; on the other occasion it was blowing directly away from it.

On both the occasions when the experiment was carried out up-wind of home, the horses walked more willingly *away* from home than towards it, although the direction of their choice seemed to be rather uncertain. On those occasions

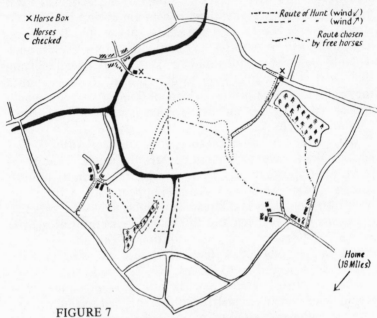

FIGURE 7

Map showing the routes taken during the 'homing' experiments carried out in the same territory, first when the wind was blowing towards home (−.−.−.) and second when it was blowing from home (− − − − −). On the first occasion, the horses, when freed, wandered aimlessly in all directions; on the second occasion they made directly towards home.

when we were down-wind of the stables, on the other hand, homing was quite plainly evident (see Fig. 7).

It is tempting to assume from these observations that the horses must definitely have known the direction of their homes when the wind was blowing from that direction, and tempting, moreover, to assume that their knowledge came from some wind-borne stimulus. One could argue that the horses' indecision on the up-wind days was due to the fact that they were searching in vain for clues; their decisiveness on the down-wind days to the fact that the clues were there. However, one must be careful not to read into the results of an experiment more than the observations really warrant. There was no direct evidence that the horses *knew* the direction of home, even at the times when they were making towards it. All that was really seen on each occasion was a tendency to walk *up*-wind whenever this was blowing strongly and irrespective of the direction in which this happened to take them. But not all horses make up-wind all the time, as I discovered from an experiment with Portia.[45]

Portia was a mare which I had trained to respond to aids on the neck and which I rode without any bridle (about which more will be said later on). Having ridden Portia almost constantly for eighteen months, hunting, show-jumping and racing her, I decided that it would be a good idea to take her for a holiday. My reason for doing this was not entirely altruistic. I hoped that by allowing her to spend a week doing exactly what she wanted to, I would find out a little about what horses do when they are by themselves. In order to make sure that she didn't simply spend the whole time standing outside her own stable, I decided to take her as far away as it was possible to do. I therefore loaded her into a train, together with several 1 in. maps, a compass, a good deal of food and a mackintosh and took her down to the West Country. Once there I climbed onto Portia's back with all my accoutrements, dropped the reins, took my hands off her neck and left her to follow her own devices.

For the first half-hour or so we spent a rather agonising time galloping up and down the road outside the station where she had been disembarked, first in one direction and then the other, but never going more than about fifty yards at a time in any straight line. Danger from the traffic made it necessary for me at last to push her off the main road onto some of the bye-ways, and once she had discovered that she was not being threatened Portia quickly put her head down and began to graze. For the first day her time was spent in grazing and resting and she seemed to have very little desire to go in any direction where there was not immediate good food to hand.

It was not till late the first evening that Portia moved away from her first position. By this time the threat of darkness and chill air seemed to add speed and courage to her gait. She walked off briskly in a Southerly direction, without any sign of her previous hesitation, up a steep hill into open country, with the wind and home behind her.

For the first twenty-four hours of our escapade, every time Portia looked like stopping for a comparatively long time I would dismount and lie down beside her keeping a long clothes-line attached from her head-collar to my wrist so that when she felt like moving off she would wake me up and I could go along with her. But towards the end of the second day it began to rain. Along with this Portia decided to set off on another of her treks. By that time we were on a small side road which fortunately did not have very much traffic. I decided to follow along behind Portia on my feet to start my circulation going and keep warm. On-coming traffic dipped its headlights and drivers turned to stare at us but Portia walked past everything without a qualm. The rain increased, Portia still walked on. The wind rose on our backs, but Portia now thoroughly into her stride did not slacken speed. Bowed under my rucksack and stumbling in my water filled shoes, I staggered after her. Several times we passed close to barns, delicious looking and inviting, but except to give a cursory sniff at various road side tufts of grass or snatch a mouthful of hedge in passing, Portia never looked their way.

Soon my feet were blistered, my shoulders sore. My hands, even, were frozen. Keeping up with Portia became a sort of nightmare. It felt like the middle of the night when at last the welcome signs of a halt began to show in Portia's behaviour. Stopping for longer at each tuft and moving on less far between them, she eventually walked firmly towards a gate and stood looking over it. Beyond, joy of joys, I could see a large wooden shack. What else there may have been I neither knew nor cared. Before Portia had a chance to change her mind, I was through that gate and, torch in hand, was investigating the haven. It was not, perhaps, the most

102

luxurious of abodes, but in the circumstances was more welcome than a five-star hotel. The door, although partly open, was wedged against the roof and quite unmovable, but at the far end some loose boards could be pushed far enough to one side for me to squeeze through. One end was full of wire netting, petrol tins and what looked like sheep-shearing apparatus, but at the other end, just short of where the roof caved in, were a few bales of loose and remarkably dry straw. Judging by the smell, I was not the first living being to have found sanctuary there. Cats and sheep had inhabited it before me and were probably there still—but who was I to question their rights? So long as they were prepared to share it with me, I had no objection to sharing it with them. It was a pity I could not have shared it with Portia too, but as there was no hope of squeezing her in through the narrow slit in the wall I removed her saddle and let her go. Too exhausted to think of lighting a fire, and cooking a meal, I changed into my only piece of dry clothing—some thin cotton socks—munched a slab of chocolate, mopped the ground sheet with my tiny hanky, and pulling it over me snuggled down in the straw. For a few minutes I lay listening to the rain against the side of my shelter and to Portia munching and snorting outside. Then I was asleep.

It was 5.00 a.m. when I woke up, cold and stiff, but remarkably refreshed. The rain at last had stopped, but a thick fog covered the countryside. There was no sign of Portia in the immediate vicinity, so girding myself for action I set off in search of her. I had not gone far before the horrid truth dawned on my bemused brain and made me pull up with a start. We were on the verge of a virtually limitless moor—Portia might be anywhere.

A survey of the immediate neighbourhood provided no comfort. To the West the ground narrowed first to a little cleft between two hills and then widened out to another vast expanse. To the North, the direction from which we had come, there were various hedges, but none of the gates in these were shut. To the South, mist and fog still obscured the view. Walking across this moor after the rain was rather like wading through a pond knee deep. My last dry socks were now soaked, my blisters stung. Despite exercise, my feet would not warm up. I stood in the middle of the mist and moor and despondently lit a cigarette.

"Well, you're not going to get anywhere doing this", I said to myself at last. "If you really know your horse as well as you think you do, you'd know where it was likely to be. What sort of place would Portia choose? Which way would she be heading?"

Of course, she had been heading due South, with the wind dead behind her, and so as she was not likely to have changed her mind about that in a hurry she would probably be to the South of me now. It was the sweet young grass on the high ground rather than the coarser vegetation of the valleys that had appealed to her all along, and, moreover, as she showed no tendency to move fast, she was not really likely to be far away. I took a long pull at the cigarette and started zigzagging through the mist in the direction indicated by these arguments. Beyond a small rise, not 500 yards from my own shelter but hidden by the fog and terrain, I stumbled out of the mist on to another hut, surrounded by bright green grass and centred by a water-tank. There, sheltering from the wind, and still sound asleep, were thirty to forty sheep, and among them, monumental in her beauty, Portia.

Leaving her to finish her night's sleep while I made myself a drink, I was just about to start loading her up when a shepherd and his dog, appearing suddenly out of the mist, threw panic into our little gathering. Sheep and Portia flew away together, and I was just wondering for a second time whether I had seen the last of my horse forever when a new and fascinating thing emerged. However upset she was, however fast she went, Portia never galloped beyond the boundaries of the little territory she had explored the night before—a territory bounded by invisible lines fifty yards to the right and left of her shelter and mine. To and fro in this area she galloped, but always at the end of it she turned back and retraced her steps, until at last, tiring of the game and deciding that there was no need for fear, she came up to me suggesting that we should continue on our way together.

I am not the first—or only—person to have struck an

apparent impasse in my attempts to discover how horses 'home'. Bernard Grzimek, one of the most thorough and prolific students of horse behaviour, carried out a series of trials similar to mine, but his horses, like Portia at mid day, did little more than saunter along the country lanes eating their fill of whatever grass they found. The sensory cues actually relied on by horses to guide them home still remain a mystery; and the fact that they tend to make their way up-wind when in comparatively familiar surroundings but down-wind when in strange territory may have a parallel in the tendency of some animals to move up-wind when hunting but down-wind when being hunted.

However, a tendency to wander up- or down-wind suggests a reliance on wind-borne stimuli, and dependence usually reflects acuity. Because scents can be carried great distances and sensed in minute quantities, the sense most likely to be used by horses in their homing activity seems to be that of smell.

THE SENSE OF SMELL

For some reason the importance to horses of the sense of smell does not seem to have been considered very thoroughly by most writers. It is true that horses do not sniff the air like dogs, nor, like the undomesticated species which they most resemble, such as deer, do they show flight as soon as some potentially frightening creation appears up-wind of them. The latter, however, is probably due to their circumstances rather than to their inclinations. Animals which are kept in stables or even in small paddocks cannot flee far if they suddenly smell something frightening, and they may soon get out of the habit of trying to flee at all. It is, of course, recognized that the smell of pigs and goats will be sensed very quickly by horses and it has often been suggested that fear causes a rider to give out an odour which can be recognised by horses.

Although horses do not sniff the air as ostentatiously as dogs, however, most horses, especially young ones, appear to take a keen interest in smells. A youngster is never at home with a new person, in a new stable, or in front of a new piece of saddlery until it has had a good sniff at it, after which it often raises its head and curls up its top lip in a gesture first described by Flehmen, and now often called after him, the Flehmen gesture. Moreover, all horses, young and old, sniff at one another when first introduced.

Undoubtedly the most important use made of smell by those animals in which it is strongly developed is in the sphere of communication and territorial recognition, and it is therefore in this connection that a horse's sense of smell should be assessed. A dog can tell from a sniff at one of the village visiting points just who has been there before him, the state of health of his friends, and probably a great many other things too. The interest and understanding on its face as it acquires this knowledge leave no doubt that the dog knows what it is doing and is using scent as a valuable means of news-getting. But horses show none of these reactions, and it is therefore doubted by some people whether horses are as dependent on scent as many other animals. It is true that a young horse will often stop to smell a pile of dung in the road or in the field, but it seldom attempts to leave a similar mark in the same place. On the other hand some of its wild ancestors—for example, the wild zebras of Abyssinia—do have special dunging areas,[22] while many domesticated stallions also tend to deposit their dung in the same spots again and again. These patterns of behaviour must have some purpose; the question is what?

One possibility is that it keeps the eating zones free from contamination by intestinal worms. Frank Ödberg found some evidence in support of this conclusion. Offering horses grass from different parts of their fields, he found that they would eat any grass so long as it was not in the proximity of a piece of fresh dung; but that if it were so, it would be rejected. However, if this were the main purpose of dung-piling by stallions and zebras, then one would expect horses to be careful not to deposit dung on the areas of short, young grass which they so like eating. It is true that in fields which are inhabited by horses alone, both Frank Ödberg in Belgium[31] and Marytavy Archer in England[2] found that horses do tend to restrict their eliminations to well defined areas, but if they are running with other species such as cows or sheep, this is not the case.

But the fact that horses, unlike dogs, tend to scatter their dung over a wide area, does not mean to say that they may not learn a good deal about one another from the scent carried by it. Dogs claim for themselves small private territories in the vicinity of their dens, but they stay in these comparatively little. When hunting and courting they tend to wander over wide communal areas either alone or in small packs. If one such animal is to know what is going on among others of its own species, it is necessary for it to have regular visiting points—like the cafés or clubs of humans—where gossip can be exchanged and notes deposited. By contrast, horses are among the animals which claim and inhabit large but fairly fixed territories and which tend to wander around these in a herd. In order that the herd shall claim the territory as its own and discourage the intrusion within it of strangers, it is necessary that as much as possible shall be marked with its own scent. Hence excreta is deposited over as wide an area as possible within the territory and can be used as tracking stations. Indeed, Stephanie Tyler noted that if a New Forest pony becomes separated from its own group, it will go from one pile of dung to another as if using this means to trace the path taken by its friends.[37]

Now it is a constant source of annoyance to those who look after their own horses that, no sooner has the stable bed been made and clean straw laid down on the floor, than the animal invariably pollutes it—almost as if through deliberate perversity. The tendency is usually attributed to the sound of rustling straw or to the dislike of staling on a concrete base, but it may in fact have quite a different origin. It may be due to the horse's desire to 'scent-mark' its new territory in order to stake its own claim to it and discourage others from infringing its property. Hence, as Dr. Hediger points out, it is a mistake to believe that all animals should exist in the same state of absolute hygiene as that consistent with the comforts of man.[15] This is not to say that all stables should be left filthy, but only that if an animal is amongst those species to whom territorial scent-marking is a condition of happiness, then care must be taken not to remove all its scent when cleaning it out. As illustration of this point he tells of one small animal, the lorris, which when put into an absolutely clean cage will make itself ill in its attempts to scent-mark the whole place with the least delay, running around its cage like an animated watering-can and drinking many buckets of water in a short space of time in order to keep up the necessary flow.

In the scent-marking of their territory horses show one example of the importance to them of smell, but it is probable that they make an almost equally good use of that sense in learning about and recognizing one another too. Mrs. Woodhouse created a great sensation some years ago, by suggesting that friendship could be established with horses and cattle by means of blowing down their nostrils.[44] According to the man who gave her the tip this is a sign of peace used by animals in communicating with one another, and by mimicking the sign human beings can do much to allay the creatures' primal fears. However, if a meeting between two horses is carefully watched, it may be noticed that blowing down the nostrils is not an invariable forerunner of friendship, nor is it in fact always succeeded by amity. Very often, indeed, this form of greeting will be followed between horses by a vicious onslaught from one to the other which may be the precurser of a bloody fight.

On the other hand, it may also be noticed that whenever two horses meet their first and most urgent activity is to smell one another as hard and as extensively as possible. If one does not approve of, or fears, the intentions of the other, it will try to smell the other without itself being smelt, sweeping its body out of reach. Since the other will immediately follow suit, only the noses of the two will remain in contact. This may give the impression that they are trying to blow down one another's nostrils although the fact that their nostrils are touching is only fortuitous. I have personally found that, when allowing a strange horse to sniff me over, the hair and ears seem to attract most attention, although the breath too, probably because it carries a high concentration of individual aroma, receives a certain share of interest. However, a word of warning to the incautious! The sniffing procedure is not necessarily followed, in the horse-to-man any more than in the horse-to-horse situation, by docility and amicability; nor is the scent which they receive always apparently reassuring. Septem would sniff a person from top to toe but still back away if a hand was stretched suddenly towards his neck or shoulder. Nona would treat a human being in exactly the same way as she treated her equine companions, following up an outwardly guileless examination with a mischievous and occasionally very painful nip.

THE SENSE OF HEARING

Although the sense of smell is almost certainly very important to horses, other senses may be equally so. The experiments on homing indicated strongly that it was some wind-borne stimulus by which the animals were guided in this situation, but scent is not the only stimulus to be carried on a current of air. Sound can be conveyed in this way too, and in fact we noticed that the horses always tended to keep their ears pointed in their chosen direction, as if keeping them cocked towards sounds imperceptible to us. This, of course, is not the only occasion on which a horse points its ears in the direction it wants to go or in the direction it finds most interesting. If, for example, a horse wants to explore a certain object, it will always cock its ears towards it. If it is wholly concentrating on the will of its rider, it will keep its ears turned slightly sideways and backwards, as if expecting to hear, as well as feel, what the rider wants it to do. Indeed, a horse's ears are so flexible and convey so much expression that it would be surprising if hearing did not play a very important part in their lives as a whole.

The majority of mammals hear a great deal better than men. They hear not only over a greater range (that is to say they hear both higher and lower tones than we can), but many of them are able to pick up sounds too slight for us to perceive. They are also infinitely better than we are at locating the source of a sound in space. If a man sits blindfolded in the centre of a room and bells are sounded from different parts of the room around him, he will only be able to tell with certainty whether the bell is to right or left, before or behind him. The different directions which can be distinguished from one another by a normal person in this way are shown in Fig.8. A dog, on the other hand, can tell with apparent ease from which of sixty-four sound points situated all around it a bell sounds. Professor Katz trained an Alsatian to sit in the centre of a circle of bells behind one of

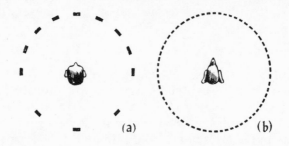

FIGURE 8
Diagram showing the different points from which a human being (a) and a dog (b) can distinguish separate sound sources.

which, unknown to the dog, meat would be placed. As soon as the appropriate bell was sounded, the dog would go up to it and collect his reward, having little difficulty in choosing the correct bell from the various alternatives. Although the dog might have smelt the meat in the first instances, it apparently found the sound source easier to localize than the smell source, for after a little while it would go to whichever bell had been sounded even if the meat had been placed elsewhere. Other experimenters have described dogs who could distinguish between points even closer together than this.[19]

Brilliant as are dogs in contrast to man, their sense of hearing is still poor compared to that of bats. In bats hearing is so specialized that it is used by them for navigation. As a bat flies it emits frequent very high-pitched cries which are echoed back to it from the objects in its path. From the

110

direction and nature of the echo the bat can tell not only how close it is to any object but also what the object is.

Although hearing in horses may not be as acute as that in dogs or bats, it still appears to be pretty good, and the speed with which a young horse learns to obey the human voice is often very impressive. I remember once long ago overhearing a conversation between two people out hunting in which they were discussing the method of breaking-in used by a local exponent. The fact that the man had his horses, within a week, obeying verbal commands to walk, trot and canter on the lunge was regarded as something phenomenal and was attributed by those who were discussing it to the force of the trainer's personality. At the time I might have agreed with them and did in fact join in silent and unexpressed admiration of the pundit's skill. However, since then I have found that horses will do the same for me and my assistants in only a few hours and have reluctantly come to the conclusion that strength of personality and character have little to do with it. The fact is merely that if the same words are repeated in the same tone of voice at frequent enough intervals, and are always accompanied by the same effects, the horse very soon learns to obey the sound. Being, in such situations, spared the distraction of an agitated and insecure rider and the discomfort of instruments imported by the latter for his aid (such as bits, spurs, whips), it is not surprising that the horse learns quicker under these conditions and is more willing to co-operate than when being ridden.

It is hardly necessary to add that not only the word but also the tone of voice in which a command is given must be kept constant if the animal is to learn what it means. For it is not, of course, the word as such that it recognizes and associates with the act, but rather the general sound. The single word 'stop', jerked out short and sharp, is quite a different command and will have quite a different significance from a long drawn out 'st-o-o-p' or the word 'stop' fitted into a long sentence and surrounded by other words, such as 'There's a good boy, stop when I tell you'. Not only the word but also the inflection becomes part of the signal.

111

Anyone who doubts this can try saying to his dog 'good boy' in the sort of growl usually kept for reprimands and 'bad dog' in the tone usually employed for coaxing. At the former the dog will go away cringing and at the latter run forward to be patted.

However obvious this may seem, it is often surprisingly difficult to keep unwanted inflexions and expressions out of the voice at critical moments, and it is probably largely through these that horses sense the anger, irritation or excitement of the person in charge of them. Very often the human being himself may not realize that the inflexion is present and will be staggered and indignant if told that it is. But if a difference in pitch can be recognized by another man, one can be sure that it will have been picked up by a horse.

In view of the undoubted quickness with which horses learn to distinguish verbal commands, it may seem surprising that they do not learn to come, like dogs, when they hear their names. If a group of horses is grazing together and one is called, it never shows any special sign of recognition; nor, if a stable is entered and a particular horse's name is mentioned, will there be a single individual response. Admittedly, the clang of a bucket will cause all heads to be raised and will arouse generalized whinnies of expectancy. But no single whinny will sound for a single bucket; no single horse comes forward to a single name.

At one time I thought this might be because horses were not used to hearing their own names as often as dogs and had not been trained to recognize themselves by name. I therefore decided to see if it would be possible to train horses to know their own names and to come to them for food. The guinea-pigs in this experiment were Peter, the red-roan pony, and Swanny, the three-year-old hunter mare. These two had been running out together for several months during the winter when the experiment was carried out, and they were being fed with corn and hay daily. They were very friendly, quiet, and got on well together.

Every morning during the weeks the experiment was being carried out, I would go into their field with ten slices of

112

carrot in my pocket, five slices for each horse. I would call the name of one first and continue calling it with the same intonation until that animal finally came to me for its reward. Once this had been received, I would call the other in the same way. In order to avoid their learning to be fed alternately I would occasionally vary the order of calling: one might be called twice or three times running and then the other the same number of times.

The behaviour of the horses showed little variation during the course of the whole experiment. As soon as I entered the field, and no matter whose name was being called at the time, *both* would come charging up to me and would stand around, nudging my hands and pockets. The horse which had received the carrot would thereafter continue prodding and nudging, while the other, disappointed and apparently disillusioned, and regardless of the fact that his name was being called next, would walk sulkily away to another part of the field. Very often I was forced to chase some way after him in order to prevent becoming frost-bitten or avoid taking the whole morning over what should have occupied a few minutes. As soon as he had received his carrot, the second animal would then follow me about, and the process would be repeated with the first.

This arduous and painstaking procedure was continued for about three weeks, but as at the end of that time it was impossible to see that there had been any progress or to detect the slightest signs of learning, I decided to abandon the attempt. In contrast to the obtuseness of these horses, three small dogs—two miniature poodles aged three-and-a-half years and nine months respectively and one six-month-old terrier—learned to respond to their names, in a single evening. A chair was placed in the centre of the room and I stood in front of it with a plate full of sliced liver. The name of one of the dogs would be called continually until the dog jumped up on to the chair, where it was given its livery reward. If either of the other dogs jumped up instead, the offender received a mild rebuff. After each dog had received two rewards it was unnecessary to call any name more than once. All three sat on tenterhooks in front of the chair, eyeing me and my plate,

113

and ready to spring at the first sound of the appropriate name.

How is one to account for this difference between horses and dogs? Were small slices of liver a higher incentive to dogs than pieces of carrot to horses, or did the difference lie in the intelligence of the animals? I do not believe that either of these explanations can account for the whole matter. The horses appeared to enjoy their carrots, when they got them, just as much as the dogs their liver, and as I have just mentioned, horses *are* able to learn to distinguish between different sounds very quickly and acutely. I believe that the difference lies in the total situation and in the natural aptitudes of the different species. Horses are essentially herd creatures and identify themselves primarily with the herd. A signal to one will be regarded as a signal to all, unless it has been learned under individual and unique conditions. Moreover, as has already been pointed out, eating is to them a communal and constant activity; it appears impossible for them to associate it with any sort of deserved reward, even though it may be associated with a signal.

But although horses do not come for food when called individually they may show their recognition of names in other situations. When we have finished riding them in the Summer we usually take the horses straight back to the field and turn them out. After receiving their handful of corn or apple they walk off firmly and will have nothing more to do with us until the next day. On occasion, however, an emergency arises: a wound needs treating or a saddle-mark needs brushing off which had temporarily been overlooked. As soon as the horses see us coming for them a second time and guess our intentions, they look extremely resentful and walk firmly but briskly away. At such times their different reactions to the sound of their names are intensely interesting. At each mention of hers, Nona would momentarily lay back her ears and take a snap at the air; at the sound of his, Unus will turn his head and give a slight whinny; but neither reduces its pace one jot nor shows the slightest intention of co-operating!

As animals are so sensitive to sounds and are able to

114

appreciate them so clearly, it may be wondered why so many show displeasure—even pain—in the presence of music. Dogs not infrequently howl when their owners start singing or playing the gramophone (even when the noise seems to be appreciated by other human beings) and some rats will even throw genuine epileptic fits at the sound of a harmonious chord. The reaction of horses to bands in the Show ring is also notorious. I remember once having the greatest difficulty in getting Quattuor, my grey hunter, into the ring after a parade there by a local boys' band, although she had shown no prior fear of the ring in an earlier class that day and the band had long since dispersed. On the other hand, some horses, especially those which have been trained to musical accompaniments, seem to enjoy the beat and rhythm of music and will keep time to it of their own accord. However, the individual differences between horses in this respect are really no more surprising than those between humans. It is well known that what may be balm to one is poison to another. Jazz-fiends often fail to derive pleasure or stimulation from a classical symphony; while the reaction of many other people to modern 'pop' hardly needs comment.

In order to understand these discrepancies, it is necessary to break off for a moment and consider the physical processes which result in hearing. Any sudden movement, like that caused by an electrical discharge inside a cloud or the plucking of a guitar string, causes minute vibrations in the air. These vibrations in turn cause movements of a thin skin which lies across the passage of the ear inside the skull (the drum), and these movements are finally transmitted to a nerve which is connected with the brain. Now the nerve, like a telegraph cable, can only transmit one sort of message: it can only 'fire-off-an-impulse' or 'not-fire-off-an-impulse'. Differences of pitch, tone and loudness have to be conveyed to the brain by the rhythm and frequency of the impulses transmitted along this nerve (i.e., in a sort of Morse code), and the brain then has to sort out these impulses and turn them into the different qualities known to us as sound. But sometimes it appears that the brain is occupied with other things when it receives an impulse from the auditory nerve, and the rhythm of the messages received from the ear seems to upset the rhythm with which it was working previously. When this occurs the whole cerebral system gets thrown into chaos: the individual feels a sense of discomfort. However, if the same sort of messages are sent up by the ear often enough the brain in the end seems to learn to expect them and allow for them. As soon as this state is reached, sounds which previously produced an unpleasant sensation will, on the contrary, produce a pleasurable one. This is probably why, when the individual hears certain basically unpleasant sounds frequently enough, he comes in the end to regard them with a certain sentimental pleasure. In hearing, as well as seeing, therefore, the importance of past experiences can hardly be exaggerated.

THE SENSE OF TOUCH

The senses dealt with so far—those of sight, hearing and smell—have one very important function in common. They give the individual information about things that are going on some distance away from him and so allow him to anticipate and, if necessary, avoid, danger. But before an animal can really know what different things are like—which are dangerous and which safe, which pleasant and which unpleasant—he has to come into direct contact with them: he has to touch them. Moreover, before they can reach the interior of his body they have to make contact with his external surface, the skin.

It is important, therefore, for the skin to be able to tell the animal a good deal about the quality of different objects, and it is indeed a very highly specialized sense-organ in itself. It tells the animal whether an object is hot or cold, whether it causes pain, and whether it is hard or soft; but exactly how it differentiates between these different senses—touch, temperature and pain—is still a considerable mystery. One thing only has been established with certainty. Most of the skin is actually quite *in*-sensitive, but scattered over its surface are minute spots, some of which will respond to one sense, some to another. Thus, a spot which responds to touch will not respond to pain; one that responds to temperature will not

116

necessarily respond to pressure.

What distinguishes one of these sensory spots from another and how the areas concerned manage to achieve their

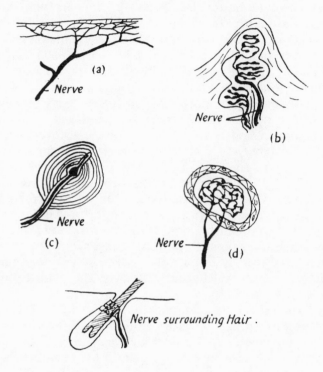

FIGURE 9
Receptor organs in the skin, as seen under the micro-scope. (a) Free nerve endings, present, in all kinds of skin; (b) Encapsulated endings seen in the finger pads; (c) Encapsulated endings found in the deeper layers of the skin; (d) Encapsulated endings found in the lips and inside the mouth; (e) Sensitive hair.

specialization is still largely unexplained. If a piece of skin is looked at under the microscope, it will be found to be full of tiny nerve-endings, some of which are surrounded by capsules of different shapes and structures (Fig. 9). At one time it was

117

believed that each shape of capsule was specialized to pick up a different form of stimulation—the oblong ones temperature, the round ones touch, and so on. Recently, however, some doubt has been thrown on this theory because, although the lobe of the ear in man contains nerve-endings of one sort only, there are points on the ear, just as on other areas of the skin, where man can feel temperature, touch and pain quite distinct from one another.

Although all areas of the skin have a certain number of these discrete sensory spots, some areas have many more than others. The mouth, the feet and the hands are particularly well equipped and are very much more sensitive to touch than, for instance, the middle of the back or the forearm. But as well as this, some areas concentrate much more on one *type* of sensation than on others. In man, the tips of the fingers are especially sensitive to light touch and temperature, while comparatively insensitive to pain; but the inside of the mouth is very much more sensitive to pain than to temperature. It is possible to drink things which are too hot to hold comfortably in the hand, although a minute pimple inside the mouth will be far more agonizing than a sore of equal size on the finger.

The general pattern of sensitivity appears to be very much the same throughout the entire animal world. The vital areas around the mouth and extremeties are always those most richly provided with sensory spots. One has only to touch a young horse around the mouth or try to pick up one of its feet to realize that this is so in their case. But sensitivity may alter with experience. In man, for instance, it is well known that if the sense of sight is lost, the sense of touch becomes much finer—not because more nerve endings or touch spots are developed in the skin but because the individual learns to distinguish minute details which he was at first inclined to overlook.

That the same thing happens in horses is quite plain to anyone who has tried to school them and does not need the proof of an elaborate experiment. When a young horse is first backed, it not only fails to understand what is required of it when its flanks and mouth are touched, but it needs considerably more pressure on these parts to make it feel what one is doing than is the case later on. Gradually, with training, the horse learns to interpret and anticipate the different signs and to respond to very much slighter pressure than was originally necessary. This learning can quickly be reversed, however, as I once discovered to my cost. Until settling down at Stones Farm I had been the only person ever to ride Unus, and we had grown to know one another so well that it was hardly necessary for me to do more than contemplate a change of pace or of direction for Unus to respond. However, in order not to disappoint the many people around the village who, on seeing horses in the field shortly after I settled into the farm begged to be taught to ride, I decided to let Unus try his hand at teaching. After he had been subjected for some weeks to the flopping, bumping and pulling of his ill-assorted pupils, I got on to him again one day myself and was horrified to discover that my aids now had to be many times stronger than previously for him even to realize what I was doing. He had apparently grown so accustomed to ignoring the haphazard thuds from heels which had slipped back or hands which had flown into the air that a faint squeeze or pull from me aroused little response. Fortunately his bluntness seemed to be purely temporary and was readily reversed. After keeping Unus once again entirely to myself for about a week we quickly got back to our former understanding.

The thing which impressed me most at this time was not the speed with which Unus once again learned to sense and respond to the very slight pressure used by myself, but his apparent indifference to the assaults made on his physique by his other riders. As soon as he learned that they were unintentional and not to be taken seriously, he was able to ignore them happily and did not show nearly as much anguish after a really heavy bang on the sides from a complete novice (admittedly he was being ridden at this time in a head-collar) as he did when unable to understand and interpret a very much milder signal from me.

This experience began to make me wonder whether, when riding, we were really giving our horses the aids on those parts of the body most suited to receive them. Although admittedly the sensitivity of any area of the skin will increase with practice, it is still a fact that with equal practice the skin on certain parts will be more sensitive to light touch than that on others. It would be as well, therefore, to make sure that when training a horse to respond to touch we are touching the areas most sensitive to it and not those only sensitive either to temperature or to pain.

That the riding aids conventionally used in this country are the result of choice and are not fundamental to the control of the animal is, of course, well known. Certain tribes of Red Indians used to control their animals superbly with nothing but a noseband and a single rein. The cowboy in Western America seldom uses his legs to turn his horse, relying more on a slight flip of a rein or on a change of weight in the saddle. Heavy horses are usually trained to obey the voice, and a really first-class polo pony will stop, turn on its hocks or leap forward in response to a rein on the neck. The question still remains, however, if touch-aids are to be used, whereabouts on the body should we touch?

Although admittedly the mouth is a very sensitive area of the body, most of the evidence goes to show that it is sensitive to pain rather than to light pressure. If this holds in the case of horses too, then the use of a bit could hardly be in the best interests of either mount or mounted. An animal in discomfort will never move as freely or concentrate so happily on its environment as one that is not, and a horse continually in fear of discomfort is not the ideal animal to ride.

The area over the ribs, on the other hand, seems to be one of those least sensitive to stimuli of any kind, from which it follows that although the use of light pressure here cannot result in much discomfort to the animal, it is not likely to be of much positive value either. Many people, in fact, find that they have to use spurs before pressure from the legs is responded to at all. Thus it appears that neither the mouth nor the flanks is theoretically an ideal place on the body to receive the aids. But if we are not to give them here, where shall we do so?

120

Some time ago I was trying to study the sensitivity of the horse's skin and to find some means of measuring it so that the sensitivity of different individuals could be compared. On the whole I was not very successful, as I could find no accurate means of getting the horse to signal whether it had felt a light touch or not. But during the course of my efforts I found that any light touch on the withers seemed to arouse a much greater response than a light touch elsewhere. It is the area, of course, which horses will always nibble and massage on one another if they want to appear particularly friendly, and I found later that by mimicking these attentions with our hands, a frightened horse could often be calmed down and made to lose his suspicions. One winter, Nuts, the big chestnut hunter who was at livery at Stones Farm, had a bad saddle-sore on his back, and every day for months it was necessary to bathe and dress this place. Being very sensitive, he worked himself into a frenzy every time he saw us approach him, and it became difficult to get within yards of him either to groom him or to dress the wound. However, we found that by rubbing and tickling his withers at the same time as his back was being touched (trying to give him the impression that he was being fondled by one of his own species), he would finally let us dab powder on to the wound and rub ointment into it without flinching. The pressure on his withers seemed to be an assurance of our good intentions and was accepted as a token of our desire to help. The use of grooming as a reward when training the pony Quinque has also been mentioned.

From these few observations, there gradually grew in me a conviction that the withers would be the part of the body where riding aids would be most effective. Not only would the aids be most readily sensed here, and not only would their application have a more soothing effect on the animal than the presence of spurs and bits, but equally important, I argued to myself, was the fact that this is an area where they could easily be applied by a rider. Whether pressure on the neck and withers would, in practice, be as effective as pressure in the conventional places was a matter which could only be discovered by experiment. It was a possibility so intriguing, however, that I decided to investigate it more thoroughly. So began a series of experiments which started in 1955 with Nona and continued throughout the next five years with other horses.[45]

Nona was a bay three-year old hunter mare, with excellent conformation and a friendly, even if somewhat boisterous disposition. Having been well handled since her early days, she was quite fearless of man and perfectly accustomed to the various traps and paraphernalia of a riding establishment. Within a day of her arrival at Stones Farm she was carrying a saddle without very much objection, and two days later I was sitting on her back. It was now that the experiment proper began. Could I teach her to go, stop, turn, back, and jump in response to aids on her back and withers instead of on her sides and mouth, and, moreover, what would be the effect of such aids on her general behaviour?

The first thing to do was to make up my own mind what the aids were to be; the second to find some way of getting her to associate them with what was wanted of her. Actually, neither of these presented very serious difficulties. The aids I decided on were fairly simple and obvious: a push forward with both hands to go forward, and a pull back on her mane with both hands to stop. For a turn to the left there would be pressure on the right side of her neck, and for one to the right pressure on the left side. In order that she should associate these with what was wanted of her, I began by combining the pressure-aids with spoken commands and with pressure on a loosely fitting head collar. So far so good. The real problem came in quite another sphere which I had not originally anticipated; namely that of enforcing obedience. Within a very short time Nona, and most of her successors in the experiments, showed every sign of knowing what was wanted of her at the different aids.

The fact that sensitivity to pressure can become very keen over some areas of the horse's body is not, however, an unmixed blessing, for it is possible that the highly trained animal may finally be able to pick up slight tensions and muscular twitches which the rider himself is unaware he is even making. The involuntary unconscious activities of the

122

body which accompany thoughts and emotions have long occupied the attention of psychologists, and it is now realized that almost every emotion, thought and desire which passes through the mind is reflected to some extent by

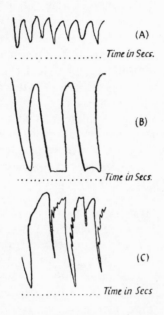

FIGURE 10
Records of the extent and rhythm of chest-movements during normal breathing (A); Surprise (B); and Laughter (C). (From A. Feleki, J. Exp. Psychol. A16, *1*, 218).

activities in the body. Although it sometimes takes extremely sensitive scientific instruments to measure these physiological changes, some of them are obvious and familiar. Probably everyone has had the experience of some embarrassing situation and has realized that at the moment of emotional tension he began to sweat and blush. Not everyone, however, realizes that the moment he even thinks of an embarrassing moment his heart will begin to beat faster, his hands to

123

sweat, his mouth to dry up, and his muscles to tense, while the more he tries to fight back these tell-tale reactions and appear outwardly calm, the more violent will they become (see Fig. 10). Even the voluntary and quite unemotional contemplation of some action will produce electrical discharges from all the muscles which would be involved if it were carried out. A person who thinks of striking a tennis ball will set minute electrical impulses passing along all the nerves and muscles which would be involved in the actual act.

Although man himself cannot detect the smallest of these changes except by means of complicated and very delicate instruments, there is no reason to suppose that some animals are not able to do so with their unaided senses, and that the very slight muscular tensions and movements which accompany anxiety, the expectation of some momentous event, or a bad temper, may not be picked up by a horse and arouse sympathetic responses in its own body.

THE SENSE OF TIME

To head a section 'The Sense of Time' might seem to be asking for trouble and criticism. How can there be a sense, by definition, without a sense-organ, yet what and where on any animal is the organ associated with time-awareness? So far, it must be admitted, areas of the body specifically concerned with the sense of time have not been found on any animals, yet the fact remains that many creatures alter their behaviour at set and regular times of the day as if somewhere within them they possessed a clock. For example, a blue fox was noted by one observer to pass the same spot in its territory at exactly 2 p.m. every day, and a porcupine was said by another to appear on the shores of a certain lake every evening between 7 and 8 p.m. for the seven years it was kept under observation. Hediger has also described how he watched huge streams of bats pour out from holes in the roof of a house punctually every evening during the month of June at 6.20, after sundry preparatory rustlings.[15] How, one may well ask, do animals keep track of the passage of time? What prompts them to this extraordinary punctuality?

As man himself is sadly lacking in the ability to judge time

124

accurately—perhaps it is for this reason that he has had to invent clocks—it is unlikely that much insight into the matter will be gained from his introspections. To man the passage of time seems to be a purely subjective affair, dependent on his expectations and emotions, his occupation and his feelings. When he is busy, time goes faster than when he is not; when he is hot and feverish it will go quicker than when he is cold. An event which is anticipated with pleasure seems to come more slowly than one that is dreaded, and in retrospect, moreover, the passing of a few seconds can seem to have taken longer than the hour of which they formed a part. Curiously enough, however, a person who may be no good at all at judging the passage of a few hours when he is awake may still be fairly accurate during sleep, and can go to bed at night with the perfect assurance that he will wake up the next morning at approximately the time he wants to.

Moreover certain physiological changes within the human body do depend on time, most noticeably alterations of temperature and sleepiness which vary in twenty-four hour cycles; and this 'diurnal rhythm', once established, tends to persist even when day and night are reversed. Hence the great difficulty many people experience after flying across the Atlantic, or when asked to change their work from day to night shifts. Yet even with these physiological prompts, man's own ability to judge time is still far from accurate. Human volunteers who have spent various periods in total isolation have always been quite far out in their estimation of time as a result of it.

The difference between the time-sense of man and that of some animals indicates that time is not equally important to all species. Is it important to horses? Most people would insist that it is. There is hardly a text-book on stable management or on the care of horses generally which does not stress the importance of regular time schedules for feeding and exercising. It is admitted that these can be arranged to suit the individual, but once a time-table has been drawn up the importance of adhering to it is emphasized and the necessity of disciplining one's self to forego a certain amount of personal freedom is regarded as one of the

125

essential payments to be made for the pleasure of keeping a horse. Because this is bound to deter a number of would-be horse owners, and because it must cramp the style of many others, it is a matter worth looking into rather more closely.

Most people who look after their own horses in the stable shut up their charges at 7 or 8 at night with a full rack of hay and a bucket of water and do not go near them again for

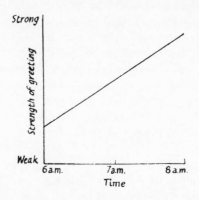

FIGURE 11
Graph showing variations in the strength of the early-morning greeting, accorded to us by our horses at different hours of the morning.

about twelve hours. At their approach in the morning, the horses will be waiting with ears pricked and will greet the fall of a footstep or the opening of the stable door with a peal of welcoming whinnies. If for some reason the groom is later than usual, his animals' impatience will be obvious and the whole stable may be in an uproar. This will be attributed to the animals having been led to expect their morning feed at exactly the same time every day, and to displeasure at being made to wait. How often, however, does the groom go *before* the normal time, and if he ever did so, what might he expect to find?

My assistants and I decided one day to see. Our horses at Stones Farm, when stabled, were normally fed at about 7 a.m. and greeted the opening of the back door which preceded the

126

first feed of the day with the customary signs of approval and expectation. Any tardiness on our part would arouse the familiar indications of impatience, and the strength of the greeting we received would be correspondingly enhanced. (Horses are fortunately forgiving animals and seldom seem to harbour a grudge or sulk.) However, when we appeared one day an hour earlier than the usual time—at 6 a.m.—our appearance was still greeted with expectant whinnies, and except that there was slightly less excitement than usual our reception at this time was very little different from usual. In other words, the only difference between a 7 a.m. greeting and one provided at 8 a.m. or at 6 a.m. lay in the degree to which the animals were apparently pleased to see us—a difference which could be represented graphically, as in Fig. 11.

This suggests, not that the animals really expected to see us at 7 a.m. every day, but merely that their appetites and boredom had reached one particular pitch by that time of the morning and prompted one particular degree of response to the promise of a meal. If woken earlier than this, they were less hungry and greeted us less avidly; if later, more hungry, and their greeting was correspondingly increased. It seemed, in fact, to be the state of their hunger which dictated their response, not the particular hour of the day.

After this experience I began to wonder to what extent horses really do keep to regular time-tables in their normal lives, especially with respect to those functions usually considered to be of most importance to them—feeding and resting. The first and simplest way of finding out seemed to be by planned and systematic observation. We therefore organized ourselves to keep watch over the nightly behaviour of our horses, taking it in turn to sit up for three hours at a time, and mark down every half-hour just what each horse was doing at that particular moment. Records of the weather, the light, outside activities,and of the movements of dogs, cats, pigs, and chickens were also kept for comparison.

We had originally planned to keep our watch every night for one week and thereafter one night a month for a year. But in the light of our first few months' experiences the more extended programme seemed to be unnecessary and was

127

abandoned. For we found scarcely a semblance of regularity in the feeding, sleeping and resting activities in any of the horses, no matter whether they were in the stables or out in the fields. One day, as shown in Fig. 12, Nuts slept from 4 to

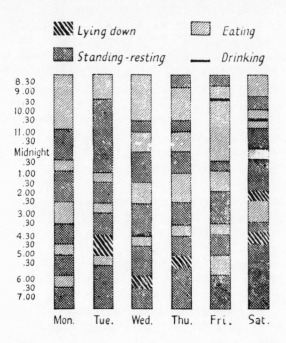

FIGURE 12

Record of Nuts' nocturnal activity on six successive nights, showing the irregularity of feeding, sleeping and resting periods.

5 a.m. and ate from 8.30 to 9.30, 1 to 1.30 and 2 to 2.30; the very next night he ate from 8.30 to 10, 11 to 11.30 and 1.30 to 2, and slept from 6 to 6.30. One night he slept for one hour; another for none at all. One night he ate for six hours; another for only two-and-a-half. Unus on the whole slept more than Nuts and ate less, but the hours at which he performed these different activities were as irregular as those of the bigger horse.

128

The outside animals were as haphazard in their schedules as were the stabled ones and tended to wander, graze or stand at rest at different times on each night. We do not believe that these irregularities could have been due to the disturbance caused by our presence, for besides the fact that we were very careful to make our observations undetected we noted a very similar variation among the owls and cocks in the distant neighbourhood.

One thing which was very noticeable was the influence of the weather. We were lucky (or unlucky) enough during our original week to strike a pretty good sample of the British winter climate—everything, in fact, from dry, cold frost without a breath of wind, to driving rain and sleet. On the dry, fine nights the outside animals grazed and wandered a good deal; on the wet and windy ones they alternately stood huddled under trees and galloped about chasing one another. It was the wind and rain, the temperature and the light, we concluded, which dictated their activities, rather than the passage of the hours themselves.

However, in the situations studied here, where food was available all the time and rest or exercise could be taken when desired, the horses obviously had little incentive to stick to any special schedule. The true test for awareness is not whether an animal *does* respond to a stimulus in the course of its ordinary life but rather whether it *can* respond to it when necessity arises. In other words, if food were only available at certain hours, would the horses discover this? Could they be trained to feed, or even expect food, at set time-intervals, independent of the stimuli either of hunger or of associated sounds and sights?

That really time-conscious creatures can be so trained without much difficulty was shown in the cases of honey bees by von Frisch. After honey had been supplied for several days running at certain times of the day only, observers found that the bees so fed only issued from their hives at the particular hours when food might be expected, spending the rest of their time waiting patiently inside the hives. The times to which they could be trained were very complicated and proved without any doubt that these insects have an

129

amazingly accurate sense of times within the twenty-four hour cycle.

We decided to use a rather modified form of von Frisch's experiment with our own horses one summer when they were all out at grass. The horses were already getting a certain amount of corn each day, but we tried to train them to expect a small extra feed at exactly 5 p.m. Biscuit tins were nailed to the fence of their field, and during the training period these were filled with a handful of corn each day at about noon. The tins were then fastened down and left in full sight and smell of the horses till the appointed hour. At 5 p.m. the fastenings were removed, the horses called, and shown where to find their feed.

During the early days of this training period the horses seemed quite bewildered. As soon as their initial suspicion of the tins was overcome, they spent many hours each day trying to open them of their own accord and retrieve the corn before the allotted time. Very often, alas, they were only too successful, for where cunning did not work force quite often did, and we were for ever replacing smashed tins, bent nails, and chewed string. However, after about three weeks they seemed to conclude that the effort was hardly worth the reward and left the tins in peace until they had been opened by a human.

After the horses had been fairly consistent in their behaviour for about a week, approaching the tins only when called and trying to eat from them only when allowed to, we decided to perform the crucial test—that is to say, to see if they would come to the tins at 5 p.m. on their own initiative and without any special sign from us. In order to test this, we had to be very careful. We wanted to be with the horses to watch them at the critical time and to see that they each had their rewards, but at the same time we did not want our appearances to be taken as a signal. We decided, therefore, that the best thing to do would be to stand by the tins during the whole day up till 5 p.m., rattling them as if about to unlatch them every half-hour or so from early morning onwards. From the way the horses behaved it would be possible, we hoped, to tell whether they had learned to expect food because of the preliminary sign or because it was the customary time of day.

Their reactions left us in no doubt. Every time they heard the tins rattle, and every time they saw us put out a hand towards them, they would walk up hopefully, sniff the tins, and then hang around, as if to remind us that we had made a mistake. From 8.30 a.m. till the experiment finished with their feed at 5 p.m. they hardly missed an opportunity.

In view of the fact that this was rather a different situation from the one to which they had been trained, however, it was perhaps not a completely fair test. We decided, therefore, to continue with our half-hour rattling of the boxes for some days, feeding every time only after the 5 o'clock rattle, to see whether the horses could learn to pick up a time-table in this way. On the second day of this procedure their behaviour differed little from that on the first day, except that they were 'had' a little less often and stood around for a little less long after every false alarm. On the third day they only came to investigate the tins if they were in the immediate neighbourhood at the time of rattling; but on the fourth day they never approached the tins at all, either when these were closed *or* when they were open! In fact, the horses were standing in the shed quite close to the tins at 5 o'clock when these were surreptitiously opened, but they did not even cock an ear in the right direction at the critical moment. Nor, when the evening had cooled down some time later and the horses walked off as usual to graze at the far end of the paddock, passing within a few inches of the available corn as they did so, did they cast a glance in its direction.

It seems almost certain from these observations that feeding is prompted in horses by signs derived from sights and sounds in their environment rather than by any sense of the aptness of the particular moment. This conclusion was most strikingly corroborated by one event which occurred during the course of the experiments mentioned above but quite independently of them. Needless to say, the general activities of the horses had been carefully watched and noted during the weeks we were carrying out these tests, and we had remarked on the fact that they spent most of the daytime standing in the sheds instead of grazing in the field. Even on days when the flies did not seem particularly bad, the horses tended to retire to the shelter at about 9 a.m. and leave it again only in the evening at about 6 p.m. Their regularity in this respect gave such an impression of time-consciousness that I was somewhat criticized by my assistants for refusing to admit to this interpretation. However, one day towards the end of the experiment there happened to be a partial eclipse of the sun, and as many of those who watched it will remember there was about half an hour in the middle of the day when the temperature dropped, the wind died, and darkness seemed about to fall. Man was not apparently the only creature to have the impression of impending night. The chickens began to roost, cows in the neighbourhood lowed for their milkers, and our horses flicked their tails, shook their heads, and walked out into the field for grass. Four hours or ten hours, the interval as measured by clocks seemed to be immaterial to them: it was once again the conditions outside which prompted them to eat, and not the inevitable march of time.

But whether one is justified in arguing from these observations that it is immaterial at what times stabled horses are fed, watered and exercised is another question. Those who appreciate regularity in their own lives and like to enforce it on others will argue that horses kept in the artificial surroundings of the stable cannot be expected to exist like the ones kept at liberty. Those who prefer a certain amount of laxity will argue that the more natural the medium in which an animal is kept the happier it must be. At the moment, practical considerations are usually regarded as dictating a certain amount of regularity in the feeding and watering of stable-kept horses, for while these animals cannot eat much at any one time they need to keep eating fairly frequently. However, the amount of food that a horse needs should not be regarded as an inevitable pointer to punctuality. During our nightly observations of the stabled horses at Stones Farm we were rather shaken to find that a medium-sized hay net and a single bucket of water had both been emptied by the animals before midnight, after which the poor creatures had seven hours in which to do nothing but await our arrival and listen to the munching of their friends at grass. By providing them thereafter with double rations at night we did not increase very much the amount they consumed or drunk during the twenty-four hours, for although they ate more before our arrival in the morning they ate and drank correspondingly less after it. Whether it would be possible to design corn-hoppers to supply food when desired, yet in such rations that over-eating would be impossible, I do not know, but I should not have thought it to be beyond the ingenuity of man. If such machines were installed in stables alongside hay-chutes and water-fountains, a good deal of the drudgery of the owner-groom might be relieved, and horses themselves might be fitter and happier as a result.

CHAPTER IV

'GENIUS', DUDS,

AND LESSONS

When a motorist draws up in a narrow lane to let a flock of sheep pass, it often happens that as one of the animals comes level with his mudguard it will take a sudden leap into the air. No sooner has this happened than the sheep following will do the same thing, and thereafter almost every animal in the flock will follow suit.

To the motorist in his car the purposelessness and stupidity of these antics is all too plain. One animal jumps for little enough motive, and thereafter, for no better reason than that it saw the one ahead of it do so, every other sheep will jump likewise. The motorist will not hesitate to class the sheep as a stupid animal and compare its intelligence adversely with that of his dog or of a monkey.

But if the motorist were able to watch the same sheep grazing on the hills and looking after their young he might have quite a surprise. For these animals, despite their irrationality and the rigidity with which they imitate one another, will have discovered just where to find the choicest grass in the country. They will know better than their shepherd in which places to lie to be out of the wind, and they can recognize their own newborn better than any human.

It might be held that these latter acts are purely instinctive and do not indicate the possession of intelligence. But this is not a wholly adequate explanation for there are intelligent and stupid sheep just as there are intelligent and stupid individuals among any other species, and the stupid sheep will never discover the best grass for itself: it may recognize such when it eats it, but it will always depend on others to lead the way.

The fact seems to be that there are many different sorts of intelligence, and a sort which is highly developed in one type of animal may not be so in another. Even two humans with nearly similar physiques, who have been born and reared in the same environment and have the same backgrounds, may actually show their intelligence in quite different ways. One may be virtually unable to express himself in words but in a practical situation (such as when the car has broken down or a gadget needs fixing) will prove his ingenuity. Another will be able to argue with the logic of a Solomon yet be unable to solve the simplest of practical problems unaided.[16]

Between these two extremes there are, of course, many gradations. Moreover, a person who is outstandingly good at one sort of thing usually shows above average ability at several others. The first-class sportsman, to the jealousy of his schoolmates or compatriots, is often a learned scholar; the brilliant artist could usually be an efficient businessman if he wanted to. But a person is seldom equally successful in many spheres as he is in one, and the good practical person is not often the one who talks best. Arguments about the *most* intelligent or the most valuable of these different attributes have little object, for although all are good in their own ways they can hardly be compared.

In between different animal species there are, of course, even greater differences than between different individuals of any one species. One type of animal lives in water and has to deal with its problems in this medium, with the physique suited to locomotion therein and only the experience of that existence to guide it. Another lives on land, while yet another spends most of its time in the air and has to demonstrate its intelligence with a body suited to flight. Each one is dealing with different problems and is dealing with them in a different medium. To assess the intelligence of each requires a separate technique—but there comes the rub: for as soon as two things are measured in terms of different standards they can no longer be compared. Weight cannot be compared with

135

length, brightness with thickness, digging with flying, nor swimming with running. How, then, are we to know whether to consider horses as basically intelligent?

The solution to the problem favoured by most observers of animals these days is to drop the word altogether and consider instead only 'behaviour' and the circumstances under which different acts are produced.[3, 17] Most acts are instigated to satisfy a need. Horses are fortunate animals in this respect, for most of their basic needs may be satisfied simply and easily by mere locomotion. Hence, it is not necessary for them to possess either cunning or manipulative skill. When it is hungry a horse only has to put down its head and eat. When it wants company it has only to move from one place to another. Satisfaction of the sexual and reproductive needs are unnecessary in many cases due to the customary removal of the need itself. (Incidentally, the superior intelligence sometimes attributed to entires, as compared to geldings, may be due in part to the stronger drive in the former.)

But there is one 'need' the satisfaction of which is essential to the survival of the horse as a species—that is the need to serve Man. If it does not fulfil this end, the species is doomed to extinction. The need is not one which, if unsatisfied, carries physiological punishments such as hunger or thirst, so it is punished by Man himself. In order to avoid such punishment, the horse must (1) *solve the problem* of what Man wants him to do; and (2) *learn* to do it.

PROBLEM SOLVING

To begin with, let us consider the matter of problem solving. In this sphere of activity two points have constantly to be taken into consideration: one is the nature of the problem, the other the emotional state of the animal trying to solve it. Thus, in the first place we must be sure that we are setting the animal a problem it will want to solve; and in the second we must make certain that it is in the right mood to solve it. Although these two aspects are rather alike, they are not quite identical. For instance, some people may be bad at geometry and algebra because they are not interested in the subjects, but are good at physics and chemistry because they see some point in them. This is the first of the above points. Yet however good at physics or chemistry a man may be, it is possible for him to go to pieces in an examination and fail, not because he lacks the knowledge or ability or an interest in the problem, but because of his emotional state.

Animals are just like us in this respect, and it is easy to mis-judge an animal's behaviour because it is being expected to do something in which it is uninterested or something outside the sphere of its ordinary experience. But it is even easier to mis-judge it because of failure to appreciate its mood.

With horses the first thing to consider, therefore, is the sort of problems they are likely to want to solve. Herr von Osten decided that in order to prove horses were intelligent it was necessary to show that they could think as we did, and work out the same sort of mathematical and logical problems as are given men. When Clever Hans' secret was discovered, Herr von Osten's faith in him was shattered. But the wave of disillusionment was probably as unjustifiable in this case as the illusion. It requires a very clever animal indeed to make the minute discriminations shown by Clever Hans in his interpretation of the nods of his attendants, and although he may not have been working out the problems set him by his examiners he was solving those far more important to himself—the problems of pleasing his owner.

In the first half of this century there were several kinds of problems often set in laboratories to assess the ability of animals. These can be described as follows:

(1) The puzzle box situation. A hungry animal is enclosed in a box, and bait is left outside. The animal must discover how to open the box—usually a simple lever has to be depressed, as in Fig. 13, in order to reach the bait.

(2) The detour problem. The animal is separated from the bait by an obstacle, some types of which are illustrated diagrammatically in Fig. 14, and demonstrates its ability by the complexity of the detour it manages to make in order to reach its goal.

(3) The inventive constructive type of problem. The

animal is placed in such a situation that it is unable to reach the bait with its own physical equipment but could do so if it made use of some tool provided by the examiner, such as a stick, a piece of string, a ladder or a chair.

(4) The perceptual discrimination and generalization problem. The individual has to respond positively to patterns of

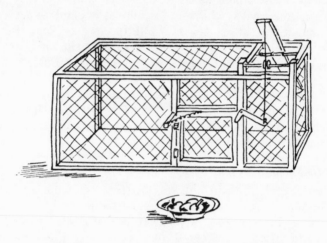

FIGURE 13
A typical puzzle box for testing an animal's intelligence. The animal is placed inside the box, and has to depress the wooden lever in order to release the door and get the food outside. (After the illustration provided by Maier and Schneirla, Principles of Animal Psychology, McGraw Hill, 1935).

one type and negatively to those of another. In order to solve the problem the individual has to be able to deduce relationships and form abstractions. This type of problem is often set to humans as well. For example, a person might be presented with a set of pictures or signs such as those in Fig. 15 and is asked to pick out from each row the symbol which is *unlike* the others. The first example is fairly simple, but to solve the next the person has to be able to grasp the idea of 'animal' as opposed to 'plant', and to solve the one

138

below he has to be able to think of 'four-sidedness' as opposed to 'three-sidedness'. In the last line he has to be able to realize that three of the numbers are multiples of four whereas the other is not.

Another type of perceptual problem can be illustrated by

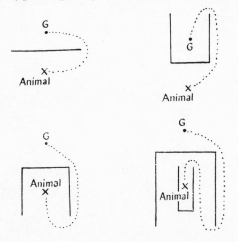

FIGURE 14
Detour problems of different complexity. The animal has to find its way from X to the goal at G. At times this entails going directly away from the goal in order to reach it—an argument which some animals find very difficult to follow.

the parlour trick of joining the nine dots shown in Fig. 16[a] by the use of not more than four straight lines and without taking the pencil off the paper between strokes. To most people the nine dots form a closed figure from which escape is difficult. One tries again and again to solve the problem by keeping within the figure's boundaries, only to grow ever more exasperated at one's failure. The task can only be accomplished if a person is capable of breaking away from the figure as it is most easily perceived and reorganizing it on a new basis—as in Fig. 16[b].

When comparing the abilities of different animals—

especially those belonging to different species—on any of these tasks, great care has to be taken and allowances have to be made for their 'natural' reactions. For example, in the

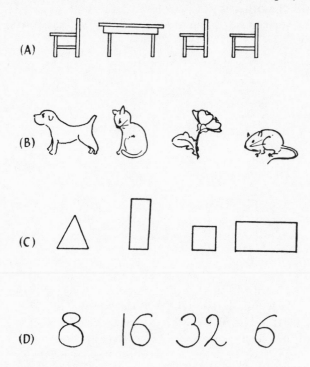

FIGURE 15
A visual intelligence test for human beings. The subject has to say which item in each line is 'different' from the others. The correct answers are: (A) The table; (B) The flower; (C) the 3-sided figure; (D) 6 (the other numbers being divisible by both 2 and 4).

puzzle box situation, monkeys and apes usually appear quite ingenious. They will sit themselves calmly in front of the catch, studying it quietly and moving it gently one way or another until it comes undone. Dogs and cats, on the other hand, tend to wander aimlessly around inside the cage, barging against first one thing and then another until by chance they happen to hit on the right part and the box snaps open. The method adopted by apes and monkeys often appears meaningful and suggests some degree of insight into the task; that adopted by cats and dogs is a hit-and-miss or trial-and-error affair and shows little of what we normally call intelligence.

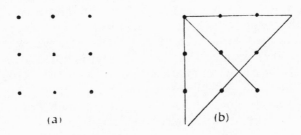

(a)   (b)

FIGURE 16
Another sort of perceptual intelligence test for humans. The subject has to join the 9 dots in (a) without taking his pencil off the paper and using not more than four straight lines. The solution depends on a person's ability to break away from the contours of the figures as it is most easily perceived, and reconstruct it on a different basis as in (b).

But to presume from this that cats and dogs are less intelligent than monkeys would be a great mistake, for whereas the solution is one towards which an ape might be orientated when hungry, it is not so in the case of dogs. Let me try to demonstrate this by analysing it more closely. The motive for escape is food. Now the methods by which monkeys normally satisfy their hunger are quite different from those employed by dogs. Monkeys live in trees from which they pick the fruit. They eat nuts, breaking open the shells and picking out the kernels with their fingers and teeth. In other words, monkeys satisfy their hunger by using their hands and manipulating objects. But cats and dogs do not. They satisfy their hunger by hunting and by the exercise of

141

the whole body. They dash around the countryside just as they dash around inside the puzzle box, and they use their noses just as they try to push their noses through the bars of the cage. This being the case, the manipulation of a latch is hardly as fair a problem in a food seeking situation for cats and dogs (to whose survival it would normally be quite inappropriate), as it is for monkeys.

Dogs may not be able to solve puzzle boxes, but, like Clever Hans, they often manage to find means of getting what they want which, if not demonstrative of the type of reasoning used by us, are none the less effective. When my two poodles wanted to go off hunting they had little difficulty in outwitting three healthy and, we flatter ourselves, normally intelligent human beings. However careful we might be for twenty-three and a half out of the twenty-four hours, there invariably came a moment when the atmosphere was unusually calm or the house unaccountably clean. Then we suddenly realized that we had been fooled again and we waited resigned till two dripping, panting and abashed figures crept back into their boxes by the kitchen stove. In vain it was made a rule that they were not to be allowed out together. Sometimes the fatal slip came through leaving a door or window momentarily ajar. Sometimes they achieved their liberty by ruse and hypocrisy ('I must go out and I can't possibly do it while I am on the lead. You'll have to let me off for a moment!'); sometimes merely by pleading to be taken for a short walk to the top of the fields. The same old formula, was it? Just a matter of taking advantage of a lapse, or persevering with a sustained effort until once in a while the resistance was lacking and the effort succeeded? It cannot be just this, because as soon as we discovered one of their methods of escape and adopted a means of counteracting it, they evolved a new one. It is true that their success depended mainly on the same trial-and-error methods as those employed in puzzle boxes, but at the risk of spoiling man's illusions of his own abilities I would point out that this method is intrinsically no different from that used by many humans. The monkey in the puzzle box does not rove around the floor, banging against one wall after another: he sits by the catch, examining and handling that aspect of his immediate environment only, but he lifts it one way and another until he happens to strike the right solution, and in so doing uses a method of trial-and-error little different from that employed by the dogs. In just the same way, human beings thinking out the solution to a difficult problem imagine one possible solution after another. They form a hypothesis, reject it, and form a new one.

Horses, when discovering what actions are required of them by their trainers, use very much the same process. When faced with a new situation or a novel command, they will run over various movements one after another, beginning with the ones that have been found to solve problems in the past. Nauri showed this superbly. Nauri, it may be remembered, was Nuki's first offspring and also the first horse I have ever known from the moment of her birth till the moment she herself became a mother.

Nauri, when young, was very quick to learn what was wanted of her, but the process by which she did so was fascinating to watch. Each time a new order was presented to her, she would run over one after another, all the patterns of behaviour she had learned in the past, keeping her eyes and ears fixed towards me the whole time for the signal that she had done the right thing—a high-pitched and long-drawn out 'good girl'. As each act in her repertoire drew the response 'no', she would drop it quickly and try another. Then, when all had proved wrong, she would begin to try new dodges and it would never be very long before the right act cropped up. Once it had been duly acclaimed and rewarded, Nauri would give a skip and jump of delight—and from then on for the rest of our session would pay no more attention to me at all!

Not all horses are, however, as quick on the up-take as Nauri. Her own half-brother, Gamesman, was indeed by comparison a veritable dunce. Every new act or new situation had to be repeated over and over again before he seemed to grasp what was required of him. More often than not he would do the right thing 'by accident' as it were, giving the impression that he had grasped what was wanted but the next day or some days later behave again as if the previous lesson had never been given.

The only true difference between reasoning as exhibited by man and problem-solving by trial and error as demonstrated by Nauri is that in the former the hypotheses are tested with 'the mind's eye', whereas in the latter they are tried out in practice.

When dealing with horses, then, the first necessity is to find problems suited to their normal environment and to their physical constitutions. As has already been mentioned, such problems do not involve the working out of mathematical laws or the learning of a phonetic language. Nor, on closer examination, are any of the classical tests which have been described above really well suited to their mode of life. The horse is not built to be constructive; he is built to run and jump. Because some horses have been known to use their teeth or forefeet on occasions, and because they have done so to open gates or doors, it does not follow that such acts demonstrate intelligence. They are probably as fortuitous as the random struggles of the dog in the puzzle box, and although an intelligent horse may realize, after he has hit upon such an act, that he is on to a good thing, and make capital out of his discovery, he is no more or less likely to discover it in the first place than is a dunce. Moreover, horses often pick up chains, rattle buckets, and pull strings not for any ulterior motive but rather in an air of play. At Stones Farm we had chains just inside the loose-box doors which could be slung across when mucking-out or grooming to allow the entry of additional light and air. In the early days these were fixed in a very carefree way on to upturned nails, and although some horses would stand quietly behind them and treat them with the desired respect, we soon learned that our fixtures were quite inadequate for others, in whom they appeared to arouse an immediate urge to play. Even after the chains had been fixed in a way to prevent such antics resulting in liberty, this tendency to toss and shake them continued in many of our charges.

At first sight the detour type of problem might appear more suited to horses, but this has definite disadvantages in countries where horses are taught to jump and where almost the entire schooling of the animal is devoted towards making it go over obstacles which it could perfectly well go round. There is always the difficulty of knowing whether a horse which fails to see its way round a detour is obeying its intellect or its training.

It is true that a horse loose in the field (such as X in

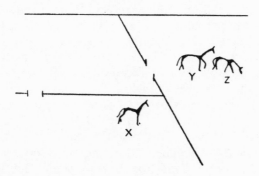

FIGURE 17

A type of detour problem which horses frequently encounter. X, which has inadvertently become separated from its companions Y and Z, is unlikely to see the obvious way back to them through the open gates. Unless it encounters the gaps in the course of its random galloping, it will probably try to rejoin Y and Z by jumping the intervening hedge at the nearest point to them.

Fig. 17) when separated from his friends (Y and Z), may apparently show almost unbelievable stupidity in finding his way back to them. Even if gates adjoining X's field to that occupied by the others are wide open, so that by retracing his steps a little way X could be reunited with his friends without difficulty, he will very seldom realize this simple solution to his predicament. More often than not he will charge up and down the fence closest to the others, pushing against it, stumbling into it, crying out his misery, until perhaps in desperation he will start galloping wildly in all directions and finally hit upon the open gate by accident.

In the eyes of most men this performance would appear to be very 'stupid', but after considering the horse and his normal reactions, X's antics may perhaps be forgiven. In the first place, as has been pointed out in a previous chapter, horses may literally not see gaps as clearly as we do ourselves. But in the second place it must be remembered that a horse's natural way of solving problems of this nature *is* by running and jumping. If, therefore, X resorts to such practice when faced with the problem of joining his companions, he is not necessarily being foolish but only horse-like.

Moreover, I have seen horses that undertook such tasks with every possible sign of forethought and insight, as was the case in the grey cob, Octavius. When Octavius first arrived at Stones Farm, he was turned out in the field occupied by Quinque and Septem, one end of which had been wired off as a pig-run. About half-way down the wire fence there was a prolific apple tree which at that moment formed a great attraction to both pig and horses. Septem and Quinque were grazing beneath it when Octavius was first let loose, and immediately after the preliminary introduction they returned to their meal of windfalls. When Octavius went to join them, however, there was a quick scuffle and the newcomer was forced without ceremony over the wire, into the pig-run. One end of this run was open at the time, and had Octavius wanted to he could have gone round through the open gate to get back into the field. But for some time he showed no desire to move, and it was not until the other horses walked off that he became restive. He then lifted his head and walked up to the wire to look it over. After a few seconds' contemplation, during which he apparently decided that he really desired to join the others, he turned round, broke into a trot, took a wide circle and, approaching the wire as collectedly as if he were being ridden, popped over it in exquisite style.

Blindness of an apparently similar stupidity can also frequently be seen in horses when they are homing. From the description of their behaviour during the experiments we carried out on this subject and from the diagrams demonstrating our rides in Chapter III (Figs. 6 and 7), it may have

146

been noticed that on several occasions the horses tried to go down side roads or made straight for hedges which, although in the direct route for home, were to us quite obviously dead-ends. The fact that the horses did not appear to foresee that they would only have to retrace their steps might at first sight appear to be blatantly foolish. But it must be remembered that when homing the animal's first objective is to keep 'on the beam', whatever that may be. Vision does not apparently enter into the job, and there is therefore no reason why the horse should use his eyes to inform him about where he is going. It is time enough for him to deal with obstructions when he actually reaches them, and it must be remembered that, despite our own superior foresight and logic in this respect, we can only reach our destination in the end by means of technical aids such as maps or compass. Hence it is not in the usual laboratory tests that horses are likely to excel.

While it may well be accepted that horses should not necessarily be judged stupid on account of their inability to solve problems of the usual laboratory test type, it might still be held that their inability to generalize what has been learned in one situation to a wider context is inexcusable. Quinque's fear of the pig Betsy; Nona's fear of the painted hurdles; Gambit's fear of the white-washed oil drums might seem to us examples of crass stupidity. Surely, we could argue, if a thing is found to be inoffensive in one situation, it must be inoffensive in all. But in the world of the horse this is not necessarily the case. Things *do* change. Man can be a friendly, helpful companion one moment and a bully the next. He can be reassuring on one occasion and threatening on another; submissive one day and dominant another. Even the fields and country over which the horse roams are constantly changing. Plants which are safe to eat one day are poisonous on another. For survival, the horse has to be able to recognize small differences which are the key to this knowledge. It has to be able to discriminate, not necessarily generalise, and this is exactly what it can do very well. It is in discovering how to negotiate different sorts of obstacles, in finding out what things can and what cannot be jumped, in developing the skills to negotiate different types of terrain that the horse's ability should be judged; and here, as most horsemen know, big individual differences do exist.

One of the situations where this is most obvious is the Cross-Country course. Here different obstacles and different situations are being encountered the whole time. No two fences are ever exactly the same or will be met in the same way on two different occasions. Yet the clever horse learns to pick his way over them all, climbing a piece of timber that he cannot jump clean, and bracing himself to land half-way down the bank of a ditch that he cannot clear. He will jump safely off cobble stones on to the verge of a road with only two feet of grass to give him a foot hold and will thrust his way through a bull-finch (a high, hairy sort of fence), or scramble over a boggy hole without hurting himself. He will not only get to the end of the course but will do so with the least possible expenditure of effort. When he comes to a field of heavy going where an inexperienced or foolish animal will race on, the intelligent old horse will slow up, make doggedly for the firmest ground and trot on calmly with his neck outstretched until he reaches harder ground. He will still be going when the fool who raced past him is spent and he will do it keeping himself fit and sound.

The silly horse on the other hand has no such ingenuity. If jumping fast and straight has once been found to succeed despite the fact that success was scored in the paddock at home or in country where clean hedges may always be relied upon, the silly horse will continue to jump in this way. Hence when he comes to the 4 ft. 6 ins. timber out of mud, disaster is almost inevitable. He lacks the equipment with which to tackle it. When approaching a tarmac road he will jump into the centre of it with an élan which only the guardian angel of hunters can prevent from being fatal and at the unexpected drop fence he will land without any reserve of balance to take the strain. Before half the day is over he will be exhausted from his efforts and will lack the energy to jump even the smallest of fences clean. If all goes well, such a horse may provide a superb day's hunting on occasions, but he will always be in trouble, with big legs, strained tendons, cuts, bruises and thorns, and he will be out of action more often than he is in.

However, it must not be imagined from this that all horses which jump clean, fast and smoothly out hunting are stupid. A horse that has been schooled to take off at the moment indicated by his rider, to approach his fences at a speed chosen by the latter, and to jump boldly no matter what the ground may look like or however impossible the obstacle may appear is not necessarily a stupid horse. He might not be able to find his own way unassisted as well as the one just described, but this may only be because he has learned to do other things. He has learned to obey his rider, not his visual perception; he has learned to answer instantly and uncritically the aids which he receives from someone else, and not his own impressions. A horse schooled like this may well provide as enjoyable a ride out hunting as his self-taught companion, but whether he does so or not will depend on his rider and on the way that he is piloted, not on his own appraisal of the situation. To expect such a horse to be as reliable and surefooted without assistance as the 'huntsman's friend' would be like expecting a classical scholar to build a bridge.

Moreover it must not be imagined that all horses who play up at the prospect of a gallop or at the sight of hounds, or who dance about on two legs in the middle of the road and paw the ground are necessarily stupid. This sort of behaviour is not dictated by the intellect but by the emotions (over which the intellect has little control) and excitement can make a fool of anyone. It affects the power of judgement so that comparisons are swept aside and an animal may act with as little forethought as an idiot. A clever old horse may be so carried away by excitement that it will try to take on fences which its better judgement would normally tell it are ridiculous while the novice may refuse something quite trivial which it would normally hop over without trouble. This was the case once with Quinque. Before Quinque came to live in the safe Midlands, it will be recalled that she was nearly drowned by floods in the Thames valley, and although this experience did not seem to have affected her nerve in general she was for a long time abnormally frightened of water. She

149

would make a quite unnecessary fuss if asked to walk along a bridge over a flowing river or cross any small deep ditch. Gradually she got used to the puddles, bridges and ditches around Stones Farm itself and paid them little attention; but early in her first season's hunting we came across a small stream in front of a gateway which it was necessary to ford. Although she had just previously been leaping hedges, rails and stone walls with the confidence of an old hand, this little ford was just too much for her. She would not go near it. The intelligent care with which she usually approached a new or potentially frightening situation vanished. She spread out her legs, stuck up her nose, and would not go within five yards of the brink. In vain I kicked, patted, coaxed, and finally beat her. In vain others tried to show her how easy it was to go through by walking ahead, and how dangerous to stay, by lashing her from behind. When a horse—even a small pony—really decides not to budge, there is little man can do about it.

As we had already done nearly as much that day as I thought good for Quinque, I decided to wait by the ford till she pulled herself together. Gradually all our would-be assistants dispersed, the sound of the hunt faded, and small birds came back into the hedge beside us. Quinque's muscles began to relax. Her head dropped, her ears pricked, and at last she began sniffing the ground at her feet. Then, one hoof at a time was tentatively moved nearer the ford. She put her nose into the water and blew through the ripples. Once more for a moment her courage failed her, and she swung round away from the brink; but with very little further persuasion she walked up to it, gave a little jump into the middle of the stream and was through. At the height of her excitement she had been quite unable to approach the water rationally or see it as anything but an off-shoot of the flood. Not till all the distractions had vanished could she put her critical mind to it and examine it with what we would call in ourselves the cold eye of reason.

LEARNING

From what has just been said it will be clear that problem

solving depends to a very large extent on past experiences. Indeed, the point at which problem solving stops and learning begins is almost impossible to define. Take, for instance, the situation of the animal in the classical puzzle box (Fig. 13). All it has to do in order to escape is to press down the lever and swing open the door. Now as has already been mentioned, human beings in such situations will usually sit down quietly to examine the catch in order to find out how it works. Although they may make several tentative trials and different movements, they will analyse their failures as well as their success, with the object of discovering the basic principle of the mechanism. Once this has been found—even if it was not discovered spontaneously but had to be demonstrated by an outsider—the human being will grasp the idea and at the same time get a pleasant flash of insight commonly known as the 'Aha'-feeling. If put in the puzzle box a second time he will have no difficulty: the catch will be opened at once.

But cats and dogs do not behave like this. They bump about blindly inside the box until by chance they happen to push against the lever and the door swings open. They do not seem to be interested in principles. Their solution appears to be quite fortuitous, and their only consideration for the bait. Yet if such an animal is put back into the puzzle box again it may be noticed that despite this attitude it will tend to hit against the lever and open the door more quickly than at the first attempt. The third time it will open the door more quickly still, and the fourth time quicker even than that. Finally there comes a moment when the animal is no sooner inside the box than it dashes to the lever and depresses it. Its escape during this final stage is just as quick and effective as that of the human or the monkey with insight.

Why and how trial and error learning leads to such efficient ends is still rather a mystery. It was suggested by Thorndike,[36] one of the first psychologists to study learning, that each time a movement leads to success, and therefore pleasure, there is a greater tendency to reproduce it in the future, whereas each time it leads to failure or displeasure the tendency to reproduce it is decreased. To put it shortly,

'Pleasure strengthens, and displeasure weakens'.

However the situation seems really to be much more complicated than this, and many different types of end result may serve to reinforce the acts which produce them. It has also to be recognised that much learning goes on at a level quite unknown to or controlled by the conscious mind. Learning of this type is found in all grades of animal life and is still far from being completely understood. Nevertheless examples of this lower level learning are worth considering.

Habituation

A snail is stretched out comfortably on a lettuce leaf, with head and tail protruding from the shell and horns raised, when an enquiring scientist after watching it for some time taps the lettuce leaf with his finger. Immediately the snail withdraws into its shell, anticipating danger. However, when nothing further happens the snail gingerly protrudes its head and tail again. When it is once more comfortably out-stretched, the scientist taps the leaf a second time. The snail draws back into its shell again, but this time it reappears after a rather shorter interval. At the third tap it does not retreat quite so far, and at each subsequent tap it retreats a little less and reappears a little quicker. Finally, the scientist can shake the lettuce leaf quite hard and the snail pays no attention. It has become *habituated* to the movement and has *adapted* itself to the change in its surroundings.[18]

All animals are making adaptations such as this throughout their lives. Indeed, were they not able to do so, they would very soon perish, for the world is always changing, and events which were comparatively innocuous at one moment may suddenly become more dangerous, just as those which heralded great disaster at one time may not do so for ever. In order to be able to exist in such a world, living beings must be able to modify their behaviour continually. They must be able to adapt or become habituated to many different forms of living.

But it is not only the mind which adapts itself and becomes habituated to unfamiliar events. The body does so too. It gets very used to being treated in a certain way and

152

resents sudden changes in the treatment. If the hair is always parted on one side, for instance, and has suddenly to be changed over, the experience can at first be quite uncomfortable. However, after a little while the discomfort lessens, and finally the body becomes so adapted to the new conditions that it even resents a change back. If a person has to have a limb immobilized, the inconvenience is at first intense. But after quite a short time the patient makes allowances for the restriction, and when the limb is freed after a few months he may find that he has almost forgotten how to use it.

The speed with which the mind and body habituate themselves to certain sights and sounds is amazing, and accounts for a good many of the idiosyncracies of individual behaviour. However, the story of habituation does not end here, for although adaptation is going on to some extent the whole time and in every one of us, it can be impeded or broken down very easily too.

Let us go back to the snail on the lettuce leaf—the classical example of habituation—to demonstrate this fact. We left the scientist shaking the leaf violently, with the snail paying no attention to his antics. But suddenly a whistle is blown or a car hoots in the vicinity. The snail ignores this noise as such, but the next time the scientist touches the leaf it draws back into its shell almost as quickly as on the very first occasion. The 'extraneous' stimulus has had the effect of removing all the habituation and of releasing once again the early, primitive response.

Similar instances of such disinhibition can be seen in the animal world every day and will be very familiar to almost everyone. A young horse that has been schooled to overcome a certain fear will suddenly become frightened again if he meets the object of his antipathy in a strange situation. Like the snail, he will revert to the more primitive patterns of behaviour and will have to become habituated afresh in the different circumstances. The effect of such extraneous stimuli must always be borne in mind, and a person should never think that his horse has been fully schooled until its learning has been tested in a great variety of conditions.

153

If an animal sees or smells food, its mouth, as is well known, begins watering. This occurs quite automatically, due to what is called a reflex action, so that when the animal finally eats the food, the digestive processes will be ready to deal with it. Pavlov sounded a bell a few seconds before he gave a dog a piece of meat, and continued to sound the bell and feed the dog in this way for some time. He discovered what we now almost take for granted; that the dog quickly came to associate the sound and the food, and that as it did so its mouth would begin to water at the sound of the bell and in the complete absence of food.[32]

Now the flow of saliva only takes place to assist digestion. It can serve no useful purpose in connection with listening to a bell; yet because the bell and the food appeared closely together in the past, the flow of saliva which becomes associated with the sound has ceased to be connected with the presence of promise of food alone. It has become what Pavlov called a 'Conditioned Reflex'.

Conditioning, like habituation, is so much a part of an animal's everyday existence, that instances of its occurrence will be familiar to all. Many fears, habits, likes and dislikes can probably be traced back to events associated in this way.

In the case of Pavlov's dogs, the response (salivation) had first to be aroused by its appropriate or unconditioned stimulus (food) before it could be associated with its conditioned stimulus (bell). But not all behaviour changes or learning follow this pattern. Learning can take place if the bell precedes the appearance of the food. Skinner placed animals (most often pigeons) in small cages fitted with a key attached to a food tray. When the key was pressed, a pellet of food fell into the tray. The pigeon was thus rewarded every time it pecked the key in rather the same way as Thorndike's animals were rewarded for escaping from the puzzle boxes. Instrumental conditioning, as this form of learning is called, can also occur at a purely unconscious level. Animals, including men, can alter their heart rates, and even their blood-pressures, if rewarded or punished for doing so.

154

Habituation and conditioning are both dependent on the consistent and repeated association of a series of events. The lettuce leaf is tapped and nothing terrible happens. The bell sounds and along comes dinner. Were something to happen so that this association ceased, so that the dinner did not come after the bell or the tapping were not followed by peace, then the learning acquired through habituation and conditioning would be lost. The unlearned, primitive responses to the different stimuli would reappear and the animal would be back to where it was before.

Besides these types of learning, however, some animals will alter their behaviour permanently and irrevocably after one single perceptual experience even though this may not be remembered in itself, and though it may be unaccompanied by reward or punishment. Such learning, first recognized by the zoologist Lorenz, has been called by him 'imprinting'.[27]

Imprinting is most frequently seen, and has been studied most systematically in birds, especially those which raise their young in exposed places and whose chicks, in order to survive, have to learn much in a short space of time. Besides arranging that these chicks shall not be hatched until they are in a relatively mature physical condition, nature has apparently made allowances for the speed with which they have to learn by organizing their brains to accept as parents the first objects (within certain limits of size and shape) which move across their field of vision after birth. If the object is a man, they will believe themselves to be men; if another type of bird or animal, they will identify themselves with that. When they grow up and their reproductive tendencies mature, these mistaken creatures will make fruitless love to the objects with which they identify themselves, rejecting at the same time the advances of members of their own species. Lorenz tells of a jackdaw which continually sat on his shoulder, courting his ears and nose with half-digested worms; and also of a peacock who, through having been reared in a reptile house, thought it was a giant tortoise!

Although these instances are most striking in birds, the effects of early perceptual experiences is also important in mammals.[14] These effects may be seen in much less obvious, more subtle, and more familiar ways, such as in the ability to withstand shocks, solve problems, or adapt to new surroundings. One experimenter studying the effect of early environment divided a litter of puppies into two halves, one of which was raised in a small bare pen devoid of dangers and distractions, and the other in cages filled with the runways, mazes, puzzle boxes and general paraphernalia beloved of and used by psychologists in their laboratories. When in later life the two sets of dogs were faced with problems involving the manipulation of these toys it was found that those which had been exposed to them from early life were infinitely more successful than the others.

An important feature of this type of learning is the age and development of the animal at the time the impressions are received. There always seems to be a critical period during which the organism is most susceptible to the experiences—one stage at which it seems 'ready' to absorb its lesson. These critical periods differ for different aspects of behaviour and in different species. In dogs, the critical period for social learning is between six and ten weeks of age, but for other species it may occur earlier or later in life.

In many animal species, the rate at which perceptual learning takes place also varies with age. In Man the optimal age is between five and fifteen years, and as one grows older the difficulty of remembering faces and names becomes an increasing social problem. But in horses, rapid perceptual learning is retained throughout life and there seems to be no fall off with old age.

Returning to intentional learning and in particular to horses, great individual differences exist in the speed with which new acts and skills are acquired. The differences between Nauri and Gamesman have already been mentioned. Similar differences existed between Unus and Secunda.

Unus was always quick to learn, and in contrast to him Secunda, who had to have every movement dinned into her a hundred times, was the equivalent in the horse world of a 'dumb blonde'. Day after day, week in and week out, I tried to teach her not only the elements of balance, but also the

156

rudiments of jumping. Day after day she would clout the 2 ft. high pole and rap her shins, and even when the pole was fixed and the result a pair of temporarily disfigured knees she continued to hit it with alarming unconcern.

However, in her later history, Secunda exhibited one of those paradoxes of learning which make the whole process so confusing and difficult to understand. She was just beginning to develop balance of a sort and was starting for the first time to show some signs of jumping well when she became severely ill with a poisoned leg, which put her out of action for about nine months. At the end of this period, which included four months at grass, I had expected her to be worse than ever. But this was not the case at all. Within a week of my beginning to ride her again she was not only back to where we had left off before her illness, but now without any trouble she was doing things which I had striven for months to teach her before· and had despaired she would ever learn. The greatest surprise came over her jumping. Starting off again with the little poles which she had been fluffing previously, I was raising them to 3 ft. 6 ins. within a month, and within two months of riding her again she won two working horse classes and gave me one of the most enjoyable rides of my life across a stiff Hunter Trials course.

In this story of Secunda one sees what I should have been anticipating from the experience of other psychologists, but had overlooked—namely, the value of the latent period or a period of rest. One famous psychologist, William James, summed this up by suggesting that one learns to swim in Winter and to skate in Summer, meaning that the long rests between the seasons often help what has been learnt perviously to consolidate and become truly assimilated. Those who have done a lot of horse breaking may also have realized this principle when recommending, as is often done, that the elementary work, including a very brief backing, should be undertaken in the Spring and the animal then turned out until the Autumn. Whether they have recognized the value of the intermediate rest, or whether this is merely recommended from the point of view of convenience and because at these times, there being less distraction, more care

157

can be devoted to the young horse, I do not know. However, it is certainly a recommendation which would have the support of scientific findings.

But the latent period during learning need not be as long as any of these stories suggest. Short latent periods can be of great assistance during all stages of learning, and rest periods, if carefully spaced, are seldom time wasted. It has been found during the course of innumerable experiments on animals and men that a thing which cannot be learned in under ten trials, if these are given immediately one after the other, can often be learned in half that number of trials if the lessons are spaced out. Moreover, the skills and knowledge acquired during these spaced trials are much more likely to be remembered over long periods than those that are acquired during a concentrated attack. During some work that I was doing on the study of memory I once carried out some experiments with human beings. My subjects had to remember long lists of word-pairs, such as dog-cat, house-castle, station-religion; the lists were read over and over again to them until they had learned the pairs by heart. Some of the lists were read over and over during the course of a single afternoon until the subjects had learned their quota, but others were read out once a week only during successive weeks until learned. About a month or so after it was all over I met a number of these subjects again and asked them, out of interest, how many of the word-pairs they could still remember. The pairs which had been learned during the concentrated sessions had almost entirely been forgotten, but those which had been read out once each week were still clearly remembered by nearly everyone. This principle seems to apply to all forms of learning and can be put to good use in the training of horses. Better and more lasting results will almost always be obtained if schooling is restricted to short-spaced sessions—if necessary two per day—than if an attempt is made to cram too much into a single ride.

But, returning to Secunda, the improvement she showed after her illness might also have been accounted for to some extent by the influence of another factor in learning besides that of the long rest. This factor is referred to usually as 'latent learning', implying that a lesson has really been assimilated although demonstration of it is still awaited. Thus, even though an animal shows no sign of having profited by an experience at the immediate time, his subsequent behaviour often indicates that something of it must have sunk in. It is as though learning were at work under the surface; as though some information were being stored, even though the animal might show no sign of this at the time.

That such learning frequently occurs in horses must be known to all who have tried to school them. The instructor struggles and sweats one day to teach his animal some simple manoeuvre—feeling that it is wrong to give in until the horse has made a response, however elementary, in the right direction—until in the end, exhausted and exasperated, he packs up, defeated, swearing to send the brute to the next sale or give it to the first passer-by. Perhaps the next day, perhaps a week later, he decides to make one last attempt. The incredible happens, and the horse responds at the first touch as if it had been doing that particular thing all its life. Despite its seeming obstinacy on the previous occasion, it had apparently been learning all the time, and it merely needed a short pause for the proof of this to become evident.

There is an important question here. Would the same results have been obtained equally well without the sweat and struggle of the previous session? Could the rider have spared both himself and his horse some anguish if he had buried his pride and given in earlier? The answer is almost certainly 'Yes'. Moreover, by packing up before tempers become too frayed the rider would not only have saved himself much pain, but would have avoided the risk of upsetting his horse too far. There is always a danger that an animal which loses confidence, instead of absorbing its lesson at however elementary a level, may resort instead to some unwanted action which serves to minimize the discomfort of the moment.

This last point is worth emphasizing a little more strongly because of its serious consequences. Any act, once it has been performed, has a tendency to be repeated and so to become a habit or a stereotype. (Hence the value of error-less training.)

But those most often doing so and most difficult to eradicate, are the actions performed in association with pain, such as in a situation where the animal cannot solve the problem which would lead to the avoidance of punishment.

I had an unfortunate experience of this once with Tertia. The little mare was coming along quite nicely and had got to the stage of cantering round in circles, leading off on either leg as required, when one day, for some unknown reason, she refused to lead on the off-fore when given the office to do so. Perhaps her leg was painful, or perhaps she just did not feel in the mood—I do not know. At any rate, I am sure that had I been wise I would have abandoned riding her on that day and tried again quietly at some future date. Instead of doing this, I got obstinate and decided to go on until she obeyed. After a little while we were both extremely angry, and instead of giving way from the pressure of my leg Tertia started slewing her quarters round into it and kicking out at the side. The next day she did the same thing, and the more I punished her the more stubbornly she kicked. By the end of that week this action had become firmly established, and as soon as she was touched with either leg she threw her quarters into it, kicking out to the side, instead of bending away. It finally became necessary to go right back to the beginning of her schooling and spend several weeks walking, trotting, and cantering in a small confined ring again before she overcame the fault and returned to where we had been before. Even then the habit was only lying dormant, to reappear once more when opportunity arose. About a year after Tertia left us, her new owner, having been unable to ride for some time, sent her back to me again to have her tuned up before she was re-sold. Tertia was in great fettle, very full of beans and clearly beside herself with the joys of life. The thought of concentrating on doing what she was told did not enter her head for some days, and at the slightest touch of a leg she would slew her quarters into it in exactly the same way as she had done on the previous occasion kicking out violently to the side. Not till she had disposed of her rider several times and had spent a little of her energy breaking various bits of harness was she again in the mood to remember what she had learned and

160

abandon this uncomfortable tendency.

It may be wondered, however, how Tertia was ever to know that by throwing her quarters into the leg instead of giving away from it she was not doing what was wanted of her. How does a horse that is being schooled ever know, in fact, when it is doing right and when wrong?

There are of course no natural rewards or punishments for such actions as walking, trotting and cantering, for backing, turning and halting, or leading at a canter on one leg as opposed to another. Whatever rewards there are, are dependent entirely on the rider, and he can only say 'yes' when the horse does right and 'no' when it does wrong. But it is not an easy matter for a horse to guess what is wanted of it with no more explanation than this. In order to find out just how difficult it is we decided at Stones Farm to try a little experiment of the same sort on ourselves, using a modified version of the parlour game 'Twenty Questions'. One of the party was sent out of the room, and those who remained decided between themselves what she should be made to do on her return. The only words which could be spoken after her re-admission were 'yes' and 'no' (not even the back-chat of the question master was allowed here). One person kept a tally of the number of prompts (yes's and no's) given for each job, and another a record of the time taken to guess it.

I should perhaps explain that besides wanting to see life from the horse's viewpoint we were interested in finding out whether there were any basic principles in this kind of learning which could help us in our training of horses. Was there one thing which we should teach before another, one kind of act that was easier to learn than another, one way of giving the prompts which assisted learning more readily than another? In order to answer these questions we chose several different kinds of job and gave our cues in several different ways.

As might be expected, we found that the ease with which the job was guessed depended very much on three things: (1) on the job itself and its relevance to the situation; (2) on the speed and consistency with which the prompts were given; (3) on the presence or absence of other cues. The job

161

of washing eggs—a not very much beloved but routine evening performance—was guessed easily in forty-five seconds and after only ten prompts, although when the same person was faced with the job of tying a knot in the tea-towel—a thing which one would not normally do—this was only guessed after the most insightless struggle as pathetic as that of any cat in a puzzle box. The interesting point in this case was that the girl picked up the tea-towel after thirty seconds and twelve prompts, but having done so she could think only of the things she would normally do with a tea-towel and had great difficulty in putting these out of her mind before she could imagine anything new.

This experience suggests that when schooling a young horse one should always start with the simplest and most obvious manoeuvres first, leading on from these to more difficult ones gradually. One should never start the day by trying to teach something completely new. Start with a familiar lesson as like the new as possible and lead on from this lesson slowly.

But to return to our own experiments, we found that the effect of the way in which the prompts were given was no less drastic than the nature of the job itself. If the prompts were given consistently and at the earliest possible moment—'yes' as soon as the person turned even her eyes in the right direction, 'no' as soon as she moved a foot away from the goal—the job was guessed with the minimum difficulty—by one person in twenty seconds with only five prompts. If no prompts were given at all and the person was merely allowed to wander around till she finally hit on what was required, the whole of her behaviour and attitude changed. She became hesitant, disgruntled, and lost interest. She saw no point in going on with the experiment. She would start one thing after another, never finishing a job or worrying about what it was. She would try to pick up cues in our looks and giggles, and the fact that one of our experimentees did hit on the right job under these conditions was rather more by good luck than anything else.

However, the most disturbing effect of all was caused by the inclusion of one or two false prompts—a 'yes' when the

162

person moved in the wrong direction, or a 'no' when she moved in the right one. Even though on every other occasion the prompts had been given quickly and consistently and though the tasks were straightforward and simple, these occasional false moves threw the experimentees completely out of gear. One girl gave up after three minutes and 70 prompts, and another after five and a half minutes and ninety-three prompts. One realizes from this how much damage may be done to an animal from even one single act of inconsistency in the early stages of training, such as patting a horse if it refuses a fence or jabbing it in the mouth if it jumps well. However unpleasant for a horse the right response may be, the wrong one should be even more so. This need not necessarily be cruel, even though it may sound hard. An unhappy animal is one that is in a state of constant uncertainty and apprehension, one who never knows from which direction danger threatens and who never knows when the blow may fall. An animal that has been hurt in the past and who knows what actions to avoid in the future is not necessarily more unhappy than a child who has burnt his fingers in the fire.

At the same time, not all punishment need be severe or even painful. It is possible, in horses as in humans, to make the words 'yes' and 'no' develop a definite significance, so that they can be used as rewards or punishments and substituted for actual acts. Horses, as has been mentioned in an earlier chapter, quickly learn to associate sounds with pleasure or displeasure, and such associations persist with very little reinforcement later. It is well worth while to teach a young horse that 'yes' means 'good' and 'no' means 'bad' at a very early stage, so that the use of the stick can be minimized later on.

During our experiment in the kitchen we found, however, that the guessers were not only responding to the promptings intentionally given to them: they were deriving cues from all sorts of other sources as well, such as the looks on our faces, the appearance of the room, or our attitude when they entered. In one case, a rude giggle as the experimentee came into the kitchen gave her the right idea at once: she ran into

163

the lavatory and pulled the flush!

That horses respond similarly to involuntary or extraneous cues I have no doubt. When we approached the stables on a Saturday morning in winter wearing our hunting clothes instead of the usual dirty 'macs and gum boots, the horses knew at once what was in the air and became restive. After they heard the horse-box being started in the summer, they behaved quite differently when brought into the stables and groomed than if they were simply being prepared for a normal daily ride. Very often such cues can be used to great advantage in training by creating the right 'set' or expectation.

But it is one matter to teach a horse what is required of it; quite another to persuade it to carry out the act. As described in Chapter III I found this out to my cost when schooling Nona to neck-aids. Although Nona learned very quickly what was required of her after each signal, she did not necessarily do it; and using the technique I had been doing I had no way of enforcing obedience. The only alternative to being a complete passenger was to use some method of punishing her for disobedience. Regretfully and full of shame, I therefore spent some time schooling her in a bit (which was used to give her a sharp pull on the jaw if she did not obey an order) until her waywardness was overcome. When I started schooling a second horse to neck-aids, I therefore took great care to ensure that in the early days no command was ever given that could be disobeyed. In this way I hoped that obedience would become such an ingrained habit that fights between us would be avoided.

The candidate for this experiment was Portia, a mare as unlike Nona in temperament as could be imagined. Portia was neither friendly nor bold nor very free moving. She seemed rather uninterested in most of the things that went on around her, and was not in the least anxious to please her handler.

During our early training sessions, I took care never to give an order until I had her full attention and until I thought she was in the right mental state to do what I wanted. As I saw she was beginning to tire I would say 'Whoa'; as I felt her gird herself for action, I would say 'Walk on'. All her first lessons

164

took place in one corner of the field fenced off with sheep hurdles as a corral, and I kept reins attached to the side D's of her head collar with which I could gently pull her head in the required direction.

Portia's introduction to the great wide world, although slow, met with no major set-backs, and within the space of two years she had won a number of Show Jumping competitions, had had a full season's hunting and run in a point-to-point.

But it was not only the mare who learned from our activities together. I myself had also learned a great deal, particularly (1) the need to make my signals unmistakably clear; (2) the need to take Portia's own inclinations into consideration before she was ever asked to do anything. I say 'asked' intentionally, because in our later adventures I had no means of enforcing my will. Right up to the end of the experiment (for Portia, alas, died of a mysterious cholic two years after I had started work with her) I had to take care only to give a signal when she herself could see the reason for obeying it. One day as we were cantering across a wide open field, I wondered what would happen if I suddenly and for no reason at all gave her a signal to stop. I did so. Portia's ears flickered back towards me, in the way Nona's had before her, and her stride shortened temporarily, but the next moment I felt her say to herself 'no, she can't have meant it' and canter on. In contrast, another day when we were following rather close on the heels of hounds, who threw up the line suddenly in the middle of the field, Portia put on all her brakes the instant she was told to and stopped much more quickly than the other horses behind and beside her.

The usefulness of habit training to bring about obedience was never clearer to me than in the case of Nuki. Nuki was only eighteen months old when she came into my possession, but even then was excessively strong and extremely wilful. She had never been halter broken, and although like her daughter Nauri she was quick to learn the *meaning* of verbal commands, it was extremely difficult to make her obey them. She would walk slowly but surely along in whatever direction *she* wanted to, dragging her reluctant and exas-

165

perated handler after her.

Using a variation of the technique I had tried with Portia, I decided to take Nuki for walks out along the road giving her commands to walk on and whoa just a few seconds before I felt she was about to do these things of her own accord. Within a remarkably short time (in fact half an hours' exercise on five consecutive days) it was possible to give the commands and have them obeyed at moments when Nuki would not have carried out these actions of her own accord. From then on progress was fast and smooth, and verbal commands were soon being obeyed without hesitation whenever given.

Disobedience is not necessarily or always due to a competing attraction; sometimes, I am quite sure, a horse disobeys 'on purpose', as if daring the rider to assert his authority or threatening his dominance. It is as if, as I have already suggested, the horse looks on the rider as a rival in the equine social hierarchy. But a horse's desire to try out its own strength is not always due to mere devilment. Very often it is triggered off by fear or lack of understanding.

Even the most frightened animals will turn and fight if they cannot escape; the horse is no exception. But there are of course variations in the situations in which they feel themselves to be cornered and so the situations in which the fight reaction is stimulated. Gwilliam, a naturally bumptious and dominant individual among his companions in the field, felt that any restriction on his activity was frightening enough to be worth fighting, and the speed with which a flight response turned into a fighting one with him was remarkable. As his education progressed and he came to realize that restrictions were not very terrible—as his fears were allayed—his desire to argue every point with me, his handler, diminished. For the first few weeks of his training, however, it was never very far away and could usually be evoked by any unexpected event or sudden movement. Soon after he had first been backed I was riding him round the home paddock (his school room) when he showed the first sign of relaxing. That day he had moved forward, stopped, turned and moved on again as soon as asked to do so and I was so delighted that I took a hand off the reins to pat him on the shoulder. I had forgotten that to Gwilliam the touch of Man was rather like a lick from the Devil's tongue. His response to my friendly pat was to whip round away from the hand, throwing me forward on to his shoulder; and then as he swung round again over his head. This unexpected happening put Gwilliam back, not just to the state of nervous apprehension he had been in before, but to complete panic. Nothing but open battle was possible. For the next three-quarters of an hour he tried every means he could to resist obeying any command I gave him, particularly if it involved going back to the part of the field where my mis-timed pat had taken place. As the battle went on his fear gave way to anger, and instead of reassuring him I had to resort to threats and even violence before he finally gave in. Once he had realised that I was going to insist on having my way and that I would punish him if he did not obey, he became, paradoxically, much more friendly towards me. It was as if he felt that if I was strong enough to conquer him I was also strong enough to protect him. After this battle, not only in the stable but also in the field Gwilliam would greet me with a wrinkling of his nostril and the pricked ears of friendship although other humans were still looked on with mistrust. The decision of when to use the stick and when not to is often an extremely difficult one to make, but mistakes can be crucial. It is all very well to realise that whereas defiance should be punished, fear if punished will only engender more fear. How is fear distinguished from defiance? As in the case of Gwilliam the two situations are often so closely linked that one mental state can pass to the other almost imperceptibly.

As well as learning to interpret his riders' signals, the horse has to develop the physical skills that the rider requires it to perform. These are all based on its natural aptitudes, but natural aptitudes can often be improved upon by practice.

This is not the place to discuss the value of different physical exercises, but I must draw attention to a psychological factor which enters into all of them. Practice of a muscular skill means the repetition of certain acts again and again until they become automatic and can be carried out by themselves without conscious control. During the early stages of practice, however, conscious control *is* necessary so that the correct patterns can be mapped out and incorrect actions modified or inhibited. At this stage, effort is involved and this arouses activity within the autonomic nervous system—activity which is also aroused by any generalized excitement or emotion. Hence, nervousness, fatigue, malaise, or any other condition which mobilises and monopolises large quantities of autonomic and neuromuscular activity will delay or impede the learning of skills. Moreover, once learning is completed and the stage of automatism reached, distractions—especially those of an emotional nature—may well disrupt it. For this reason the mental state of the individual both during training and at the time the skill is to be utilized (in the competition itself) is vital to efficiency. Mental relaxation therefore must be fostered as carefully as physical fitness.

The difficulty is that there are some horses, like some people, which actually perform better when tense than when too relaxed. It seems that for each individual there is a state of generalized emotional arousal associated with optimal performance of a skill.[5] Tension below or above this level causes a fall-off of performance (below it, not enough autonomic activity is being stimulated: above it, energy is being withdrawn from the skill performance proper). The amount of distraction or stimulation required to produce optimal performance in any individual will depend on (1) the degree to which performance of the skill itself utilizes autonomic activity; (2) the level of autonomic activity present in the normal state. Horses which are continually and even at their quietest in a highly nervous, jittery condition, need very little extra to tip them over their optimal level. Those on the lazy, placid side which find whatever they are being asked to do almost too easy, may need extra stimulation (a new arena or a large audience) to produce their best. There are many experienced and capable Show jumpers in this latter group, and indeed it is unlikely that a horse will reach the top rank as a Show jumper unless it is normally fairly placid.

When schooling a young horse to carry a rider it is almost always found that in the early stages one side is stiffer than the other—i.e. that instead of the spine being in a dead straight line between the head and tail, it is curved sideways in the form of a bow. The usual bow is towards the left, or nearside, causing difficulty when the horse is asked to turn in the opposite direction—or lead with its off-foreleg at a canter. The tendency in favour of left-sided flexion does not seem to be confined to riding horses or even to modern times. Judging from ancient sculptures and other archaeological evidence horses throughout the ages and in all parts of the world, however they were controlled (i.e. those pulling chariots or sulkies as well as ridden) showed a preference for left-handed bends.

Possible reasons or explanations for this have been considered by many people.[6] The most common explanation attributes it to the effect of handling. Since right-handed people prefer to lead and touch the horse from its left side, it is presumed that the maturing animal will develop a flexional asymmetry in this direction. Other authors have postulated anatomical reasons involving the circulation of the blood, tension on the larengial nerve, or cerebral development.

According to the circulatory theory, as it is the left ventricle of the heart which pumps blood around the body, the flow of blood through the vascular system would be marginally assisted by moving to the left. Conversely, movement to the right would somewhat impede the flow of blood causing a slight fall in blood pressure which might handicap the individual in flight from predators. According to the larengial nerve theory, it is argued that as the left larengial nerve has to pass over the enlarged left ventricle, it is always under slightly more tension than the right (hence the fact that larengial nerve paralysis causing 'broken windedness' occurs more usually on the left than the right side), and the flexion of the head and neck towards the right will increase this tension on the larengial nerve and so place it under even more pressure than it is in the animal's resting state.

The third possible anatomical basis, that of cerebral asymmetry, has been considered by a number of people.

That the majority of human beings are right handed for the majority of acts, there is little doubt. Nor is there any doubt about Man's handedness being closely associated with his ability to speak, since injuries to the left cerebral hemisphere not only paralyse the right side of his body (in particular the right upper limb) but also his speech[47] (this occurs in left-handed as well as in right-handed people).

Laterality or handedness has been studied in a number of other animal species besides Man; from mice to chimpanzees and from tits to parrots.[1] Unlike Man, most of the species (except cats) have turned out to show predominantly mixed handedness, those individuals which consistently use one hand rather than the other showing about equal numbers preferring the right to the left (cats tend to prefer the left). To determine the laterality preference of horses, Grzimek studied the foreleg used by horses in three different situations. (1) to lead when moving off from a standstill; (2) to lead when being driven over a pole on the ground; and (3) to paw the ground in expectation of food or in generalized excitement. He found a little preference, if anything, for the right (off) fore.[10] Ödberg repeating Grzimek's experiments came to much the same conclusion.

Wondering whether it could be related to the side from which foals suckled (because in order to suckle, the foal usually stands alongside the dam facing the opposite way to her and turning its head up towards her udder) I spent one summer noting the sides from which foals did, in fact, drink. In all, I watched seventy-three different foals taking a total of 211 drinks at four different Studs. There was not very much consistency of side preference, but on all the Studs more drinks were actually taken from the dam's off (or right) side than from her near (or left).[48] Hence, the possibility that adult flexional asymmetry can be due to habits set up by suckling is ruled out.

Sometimes it is easier to understand the causes of a condition by studying not the condition itself but the exceptions to it. That there are exceptions to left-sided stiffness, most experienced people would agree. Those which stand out most clearly in my own mind are those horses which I schooled and rode by neck-aids instead of bits. These horses, with no confinement to the activity of their heads, would use their heads and necks to balance themselves much as American ponies do when cow-cutting. At the same time I noticed that they tended to maintain their spines in a curve upwards under the saddle instead of downwards as the schooled riding horse is supposed to do. In some respects it was not the most comfortable position for the rider—nor perhaps did it make the horse look particularly beautiful—but it enabled the horse to stop, turn, accelerate and decelerate very much more quickly than normal. None of the horses so ridden showed any trace of the usual lateral stiffness.

Unfortunately it became necessary to school some of the horses so trained, to the usual riding aids later on, so that they could be ridden by other people. The moment a bit was put into their mouths and their heads were brought up into the conventional position, a left-sided stiffness was immediately apparent and continued to be evident until the horses were 'schooled out of it'. Whether the cause of the change was pressure on the mouth, the position of the head carriage, or the heavy-handedness of the rider (most riders tend to carry a whip in the right hand and so are unable to flex this hand with the same suppleness as the other) it was impossible to say. Being aware of this possibility of heavy-handedness I myself carried no whip at all, or, if I had to, changed it from one hand to the other every few minutes, but this did not prevent all my conventionally-ridden horses from showing lateral stiffness when first ridden.

MEMORY

Although there are not quite so many stories in existence about the memory of horses as about that of elephants, it is generally agreed that the memory of a horse is a very remarkable thing. If a horse has once been hurt it will forever remember and avoid the circumstances. If a person has once given it something good to eat, it will continue to expect tit-bits from him.

But then, so would we, and so would many other creatures, and these instances do not really prove that the

171

memory of a horse is particularly phenomenal. The trouble is that memory is a difficult thing to define and measure, and it is therefore difficult to compare the memory of two different individuals. Unlike learning, which can be judged by behaviour, memory, which concerns only the recollection of events or impressions, is a purely private affair and can only really be judged by the person who is experiencing it.

Nevertheless it is true that some people and animals do seem to have better memories than others. They remember more events and they remember them more accurately. Moreover memory seems to be something which a person can 'lose' without the loss of other intellectual faculties. One man I met, who was suffering in this way as a result of an injury to the brain, was still able to do the *Times* crossword puzzle unassisted every day, although he could not remember anything that happened from one minute to the next. If he was shown a picture and asked three minutes later what it was, he would deny that he had been shown anything at all. Even if it was shown to him again, he would be inclined to say that if he had ever seen it in his life it must have been during his early childhood.

Yet if one analyses carefully the differences between a good memory and a bad memory, one finds there are innumerable traps. A person with 'no memory at all' does not forget everything, and even the man mentioned above could remember his early childhood perfectly well. It was also found that although he might not be able to remember an experience if he was asked about it casually, certain prompts or cues often managed to bring it back to him quite well. Again, in his case as in many others, an emotion could often be aroused by something with which it had been associated before, although he would be unable to remember the previous experience. For instance, he had to have some electrical treatment which, although not actually painful, was apparently somewhat unpleasant. The first time the doctor entered his room with the apparatus, the patient was very interested and asked several questions about how it worked. The next time the doctor appeared, however, he shrank back into a corner of the bed, saying he thought the treatment was

172

quite unnecessary. When asked if he had ever had it before and whether it had hurt, he denied both. 'No, I've never seen that instrument either, but things like that scare the life out of me'.

Although a person like this may appear quite abnormal, closer scrutiny of even the best memories shows that they are far from perfect. If a person, even one who fancies himself at this type of thing, could compare his memory of a scene or event with a cinema record of it (as has now been done in some laboratories) he will probably be amazed to find how inaccurate he is. Some details will be exaggerated while others are left out. Many will be altered slightly and twisted to resemble what he would have liked or expected. The longer the lapse of time since the event itself, the greater, in general, will be these changes, until in the end his representation or memory of the experience may be quite different from the event as it took place. Professor Bartlett of Cambridge showed his students some pictures and asked them to reproduce them from memory after different intervals. He found that small details which did not fit in with the students' ideas of what the pictures *should* have represented were frequently omitted or changed, and as time progressed the pictures came to conform more and more with the educational and cultural background of the individuals concerned.[4]

However it is not only the passage of time itself which affects the memory. What happens during the time is just as important—perhaps more so. If we simply sit down and rest or go to sleep after an experience, there is a good chance we will remember it fairly accurately and for a fairly long time. If something hits us on the head and knocks us unconscious we may never be able to remember the event again; our minds will have a complete blank for that few minutes for the rest of our lives. If, however, we meet with an accident which does not make us lose consciousness but only causes shock and pain, or if there were some sudden catastrophe like the explosion of a gas-works or the falling of a bomb, we might remember the preceding events with amazing clarity for years to come. All the trivial details which are normally

173

forgotten within a few hours—the preparations for a meal, the routine inspection of a boiler, the house-work etc.— remain pin-pointed with incredible vividness, so that even twenty years later we may still be able to say what we were

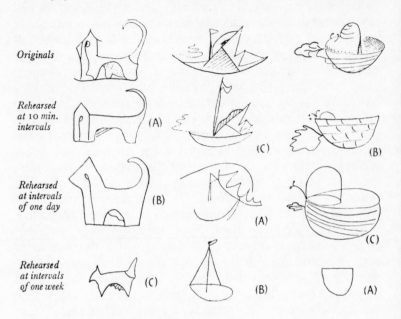

FIGURE 18

Some pictures and their reproductions from memory 5 weeks later by 3 subjects (A), (B) and (C), showing the effect of early rehearsal on the accuracy and detail with which they remembered. Those which are reproduced 4 times at 10 minute intervals immediately after being seen, are remembered better than those reproduced 4 times at weekly intervals.

doing between 2.00 p.m. and 3.30 p.m. on the day of the catastrophe, although quite unable to account for our movements on other individual days so long ago.

Our very vivid recollection of these details is doubtless due in part to the fact that we have been going over them in our mind describing them to the various doctors, lawyers, or friends who asked how it all happened. Such rehearsal certainly helps to fix memories; yet if it is to fix them accurately it must be started straight away after the event has happened and must not be left for some hours or weeks. If we try to think back over something to which no particular attention was paid at the time, our memory will almost certainly be faulty. I once demonstrated this with the following experiment. Using some rather obscure and equivocal pictures like those of Professor Bartlett, I showed these to several people who were asked to draw them from memory as best they could after different time intervals (Fig. 18). One was drawn every 10 minutes for the first hour, another every day for the first four days, another every week for the first month. After five weeks the subjects were asked to draw each picture again, and their memory for the different ones was then compared. Of course a good deal depends in such a test on the subjects' ability to draw, but as can be seen from the reproductions in Fig. 18 much more has been forgotten on the whole by all the subjects if the initial reproductions are delayed than if they are executed straight away. In other words, unless the first rehearsal takes place within a fairly short time of perception the vast majority of details are forgotten. It is after this initial period that the spacing of rehearsals has the optimal effect.

There is one point about remembering that takes some explaining. We do not keep in mind everything we could remember at the same time. Certain recollections may be uppermost when we are thinking about them or reminded of them; others are lying dormant at the back of our minds to be awoken at the correct moment. But where is 'the back of our minds'? What is happening to these memories when we are not remembering them?

Very much has been speculated on this matter and innumerable theories have been put forward to account for it. One thing we do know is that the memories which will be uppermost in a person's mind at any one moment are dictated to some extent by what he perceives at the present moment—by reminders from the immediate environment. Memory and perception are very closely connected. and since

175

we know that perception has a physiological basis in the brain, most people feel that memory must be connected with the brain as well. Whether it is stored in some *area* in the brain, whether it is stored in *coded messages* which are continually circulating around it, or whether each experience changes the *molecular* constituents of the brain in some way is not yet known, and probably it never will be known until a great deal more research has been done on the physiology of the brain itself.

It will be realized now that when we come to consider the memory of animals a great deal has to be taken into consideration. It is unlikely that the basic principles of their memories differ much from ours, so that we can be pretty certain that what and how well a horse remembers will depend on at least four things: (1) The importance to it of the event itself; (2) What happened after the event; (3) The time which has elapsed since it occurred; and (4) The circumstances and reminders of the moment. It is obviously unfair to compare a man's memory for a midday meal one year ago with a horse's memory for a train crash which happened at about the same time. A train crash is an important emotional event and is far more likely to be remembered by any creature than is one single meal. Yet when an animal is reputed to have a phenomenal memory the judgement is often based on some such comparison as this. I do not mean to deny that horses have good memories. Indeed, I have had ample proof to the contrary although I will only quote one anecdote in illustration. One day I was out hunting with Portia—one of the horses I rode without a bit—standing at the head of a lane which ran alongside a covert, because I was expecting the hounds to break in front of us. When they failed to do so and we had to retrace our steps, I decided to take a short cut over a particularly difficult part of the country which Portia and I had crossed together only once before. It involved following an intricate course of wire-surrounded, ploughed fields, boggy holes and narrow bridges. I was not sure that I could remember the way but as we approached one after another of the not too familiar landmarks I felt Portia steady herself and prepare to

176

make each turning at exactly the right moment. She appeared to be able to remember without any difficulty each one of the many complicated turns, even though she had only been that way once before and I had been there several times. The difference between Portia's memory of this route and mine can once again probably be ascribed to our different natural needs and habitats. Whereas a horse's survival in the wild depends on its ability to fend for itself and find its own way around, I can—and do—rely on sign posts, maps and helpful local inhabitants, in all of which language has supplanted direct perception.

CHAPTER V

TEMPERAMENT
AND CHARACTER

For some time it was my boast that I had never bought or sold a horse with a bad temperament. I claimed, as many others have doubtless done, that I could tell as soon as I saw an animal what it would be like, and moreover, that my judgment had never let me down. This is not to say that all my horses had been alike. I had had slugs and racers; some that always behaved as if full of corn and others that never did. Yet compared to those other horses which I had looked after for different people my own seemed to be paragons of virtue. Unus did not bite or kick like Peter. Quattuor never chased the geldings like Swanny. Old Nuts was absolutely viceless, but stolid and rather stupid. I was glad that both Septem and Octavius showed a little more life than he did.

Despite my own feelings on the subject, however, the owners of these other horses adored their property and would not have parted with them for twice their value. Peter's mistress loved her pony just because of its uppishness and obstinacy. She was amused beyond words one day when the little devil stood mulishly in the middle of the road, staring at a piece of paper on the verge, and forced an American Army lorry which could not pass her to go back and round by a different road. Swanny's owner loved the mare, despite her sexual aberrations, and Nuts' cumbersome docility did not worry his owner in the least.

Realizing how quickly and easily one manages to accustom oneself to, and even make capital out of, the short-comings of an object that is loved, I began one day to wonder whether

178

my own horses had not also perhaps a few peculiarities which might have struck others as being undesirable and unwanted. Certainly, Secunda was 'funny' in her box. She would greet all those who entered by laying back her ears and waving her head up and down as if to savage the intruder, and there was a tendency among those who went to feed her for the first time to drop the bucket on the stable floor and beat as quick a retreat as possible. It is true also that she would stand for hours on end kicking the sides of her box. I knew that this habit had developed during the time she was laid up with a poisoned leg and was rather shocked to find such tendencies listed among the vices in several horsey books.

But of course there was also Billy Bunter, bumptious, nappy, and self-willed, who, it could not be denied, showed many of Peter's undesirable qualities. Knowing, or thinking that I knew, how Billy's troubles had arisen, however, I could forgive him for showing a little spirit and for occasional outbursts of temper. Moreover, it was just these tendencies which made him such an interesting pony to ride, the very antithesis of the dumb Secunda.

Then what of Tertia? How to excuse her kicking and the way she reared when first being backed? The fact that Tertia soon grew out of these habits, however, and that she settled down into a reliable hack, indicated to my mind that she could not have been fundamentally bad. Her antics, I was sure were due to *joie-de-vivre*, together with a certain excitability and apprehension, and should, it seems, be regarded in the same way as the slipper-chewing period of puppyhood: it is an unfortunate phase, but if the animal is treated properly it will soon pass over.

In contrast to these, Quattuor, the star-gazer and sleepy-head, might have appeared to have the ideal temperament, and certainly she had many fans among the beginners. Yet there is no doubt that the more ambitious riders found Quattuor dull and uninteresting. She was so completely predictable, so utterly conventional.

The fact seems to be that a temperament which is right in one sphere of activity is not necessarily right in another; one which suits one person does not suit all. Hence, rather than talking about good and bad temperaments in a horse, it would probably be wiser to consider them as fitting or unfitting to the situation in which they are found. That this is the common practice in man is, of course, well known. One cannot talk about the typical Latin temperament as being 'better' than the typical Nordic one, although there are situations to which it is more suited. The temperament and character which fit the British way of life do not go down at all well in many other countries, but at the same time the flighty, excitable characteristics of some other nationalities seem rather exaggerated over here. The right temperament in a horse, as in man, is one which suits its environment.

But in saying this, the problem of temperament is by no means solved. Indeed, it is scarcely even clarified, for other problems arise at once. Everyone knows what sort of temperament he wants in the horse of his possession, but how can a would-be owner recognize the temperament in a horse that he is contemplating buying? How can he know whether it is the temperament for the job he has in mind? How can a breeder know what will be the temperament of a horse he produces? Finally, or perhaps it should have been primarily, on what does temperament depend?

These subjects have been studied in a number of different species, and although the answers to most of the questions are still far from complete, certain points are beginning to emerge.[8] In the first place, though, it is important to decide exactly what is meant by the word temperament itself. Most biologists and psychologists have decided to treat it in the same way as the words instinct and intelligence—that is to say they have stopped using it. Horsemen, however, still find it useful. To them it implies much the same as modern psychologists include in the term Personality; the general consistency with which the animal behaves, its tendency to do certain things in certain situations. It is temperament which causes those differences between individuals which cannot be accounted for on the basis of intelligence or learning.

Temperament has long been regarded as dependent on some property of the body, but exactly what aspects of the

180

physical constitution are responsible for the mental one is a matter still in doubt.

At one time there were great hopes that the secret might be found in the *endocrine glands*, those small organs situated in many different parts of the body which manufacture highly complex chemical substances called hormones. When these hormones are circulating around the body quite striking changes of behaviour and attitude may be seen in the individual. A submissive hen, low down in the pecking order, will, if injected with extracts from the glands of an aggressive male, become dominant and assertive. Placid, timid rats, if injected with hormones from the glands of over-active and nervous ones, will become edgy and excited. But unfortunately this is not the end of the matter, for although the state of the individual's glands and the amount of different hormones they secrete apparently affects his mood, the state of the mind can correspondingly influence the workings of the glands. For instance, it has been established that 'neurotic' rats have larger and heavier thyroid glands than their more stable contemporaries, but it is also recognized that normal rats which have been made neurotic by subjection to stress have heavier thyroid glands than their more equably raised litter mates. Thus, since the interaction between glands and temperament seems to operate in both directions, it cannot be conclusively held that the state of the glands decides the temperament of the individual.

Another aspect of the body whose relationship with temperament has been closely studied is the *central nervous system* and the brain. The fact that the brain is closely connected in the higher animals with many aspects of behaviour is, of course, taken for granted, but that it may also be connected with more abstract qualities of personality and character has long been suspected. The difficulty is to know between what part of the brain and which particular aspects of behaviour the connection lies.

In one of the first attempts to study this association at the beginning of the last century Gall claimed to have found a connection between a person's character and the different bumps on the exterior of his skull, a study he called phrenology (Fig. 19). However, Gall's claims were found to have little general application—even though he did try to apply them to horses (Fig. 20)—and the popularity of phrenology was short-lived. If Gall could instead have found some method of measuring the bumps on the outside of the brain beneath the skull, it is possible that he might have been

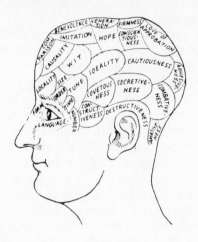

FIGURE 19
The 'Organs of the Mind', and their representations on the surface of the skull, according to the Phrenologists of 1815. (After the frontispiece in The Physiognomic System of Gall and Spurzheim, by J.G. Spurzheim, Baldwin Cradoch and Joy, 1815).

more successful, although it is doubtful whether even this would have given him much information about a person's temperament as such. It is true that a crude connection seems to exist between the development of certain areas of the brain and some aspects of mental activity, but the connection is not always very consistent, nor does it tell us much about the individual's idiosyncrasies. For example, the use of speech and the control of the right hand are connected with activities normally carried out by the part of the brain lying beneath the left temple. Practical abilities and the use of

182

tools, however, depend more on the right-hand side of the brain.[47] However, the outer dimensions of the brain, and even its general appearance under the microscope, give little indication of the degree to which the areas in question are used.

There is one area of the brain, known as the frontal area lying just above the eyes and behind the forehead, which was thought for some time to have more significance in this

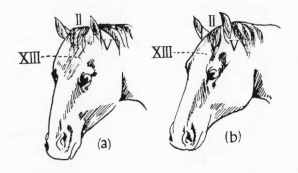

FIGURE 20
Phrenology, as it was applied to horses in 1815. Three different 'Organs of the mind' are illustrated here: II Love of offspring, well developed in (a) but not in (b); V Combativeness, developed in (a) but not in (b); XIII Benevolence, developed in (a) but not in (b). (From The Physiognomic System by Spurzheim, 1815).

respect. Although the shape and outward appearance of this area may not differ very much between one person and another, it has consistently been found that an injury to it, although not causing any disturbance of consciousness, intellect or memory, may have a profound and lasting effect on the general personality of the sufferer. A previously considerate housewife whose home had hitherto been spotless and whose children were scrupulously clean may become blousy, careless and unreliable. She will invite people to a party but make no preparations for their arrival. She will see

183

her children going around in rags and, apart from verbal complaints, do little to remedy the matter. A shrewd business man may, after such an injury, behave for the rest of his life like a thoughtless schoolboy.

Yet on closer analysis it is not the temperaments of these people that is really changed by such an injury so much as their ability to control it. The business man always seems to have been a schoolboy at heart, but realizing the inappropriateness of such an attitude in his adult work made a big effort to control himself. The housewife loathed her daily chores, but almost because of this had forced herself to carry them out to perfection. It is as if, whatever the underlying temperament, it has only been accentuated by the disturbance to the brain; it has not otherwise been altered. A person who was quiet and withdrawn before, becomes even quieter and even more withdrawn after injury. One who was cheerful, open, and hearty becomes a caricature of these tendencies. Hence, this area of the brain cannot really, any more than the glands, be regarded as determining the personality of the individual.

With inability to localize personality in either the glands or the central nervous system, attempts have been made to look for it in more general characteristics of the body, such as in the *shape* and *proportion* of its different parts. Some of the early attempts in this sphere were little more successful than those of the phrenologists, possibly because, like the latter, they were unfortunate in choosing superficial and unimportant aspects of the body with which to match the characteristics of individuality. Lombroso, for example, tried to match anti-social tendencies with certain aspects of the face and head—to delineate what he called the stigmata of the 'criminal type'. After spending a long time studying the physiognomy of the inmates in various State prisons and noting the high proportion among them of small skulls, heavy jaws, and pointed ears, Lombroso put forward the suggestion that these facial characteristics were significant of criminality in general (Fig. 21). However, critics were not slow to point out that the same stigmata might be seen in the faces of many non-criminal people and, moreover, that many people

184

with criminal tendencies and very different features might be at large outside the prisons.

However, the disapproval with which Lombroso's efforts

FIGURE 21
Three of Lombroso's 'Criminal Types', exhibiting the small, narrow, flattened or pointed skulls, the asymmetrical faces and large ears which this observer believed to be the 'stigmata' of the criminal.

were received was not really due so much to his attempts to define and measure aspects of the body as to his attempt to make out that some types of personality and temperament were more desirable than others. Although there may not be one type of body or face associated with goodness, few

185

people would deny that there is some connection between a person's general physique and some other aspects of behaviour. Fat people tend to be jolly. They do not worry about the future and are optimistic. Thin ones, on the other hand, are withdrawn, dour, pessimistic and tend to be on the look-out for trouble. Although this has been recognized even since before the days of Shakespeare, it was not till comparatively recently that a German psychiatrist, Kretschmer, decided to measure the proportions of these different body-builds and work out their connection with the different personality types on a statistical basis.[24] Since his pioneer work the matter has received a great deal of attention, and considerable efforts have been made to find out exactly what mechanisms cause the association.

Not all these have yet by any means been established, although some are gradually becoming clearer. From interviews, questionnaires and observations of many hundreds of American students, it has been estimated by W.H. Sheldon that the individuals with different physical builds have at the same time different physical 'needs', and it seems possible that the differences between personality can be explained to some extent on that basis. For example, since fat men have greater appetites than thin ones, they tend, if faced with the choice of spending their last shillings on a good meal or on going to a concert, to choose the former. Thin ones, on the other hand, to whom food is less important, can afford to be more artistic.

At the same time, we do know, of course, that the state of the mind can influence that of the body, and that a fat, jolly, carefree woman who loses her husband and begins to worry about the upbringing of her children may become thin and haggard, while a slim, tense young artist who takes to drink to drown his disappointments loses the urge to create and becomes fat and gross.

Serious investigations of the outward physical characteristics associated with personality differences in humans have so far been confined to general physique. But there is another aspect of the body, more fundamental and unchangeable perhaps even than its shape, which laymen commonly

186

recognize as being associated with individual differences; this is the *colour* of the skin and hair. Red-headed individuals are traditionally held to be hot-tempered, dark ones are said to be deeply purposeful and often egocentric. Black is the colour of the villain and the 'femme fatale'. Blue eyes and fair hair are associated with frankness, docility and idleness. Although these associations in man have not yet been verified scientifically and may turn out to be as spurious as the stigmata analyzed by Lombroso, a definite association between pigmentation and temperament has been found to occur in some animals. There is good evidence from the work of J. Keeler and others that in rats and mice different coat-colours carry with them the tendency to react in different ways. Black rats, whatever the stock from which they are bred, tend to be tamer, quieter, slower and less easily ruffled than others; grey ones, on the other hand, even when bred and reared in the laboratory, are always treacherous, wild, and tend to snap at their keepers.[20]

From all these investigations a few points seem to stand out. In the first place, temperament or personality coincides with many aspects of the body and is altered when alterations are induced in the physical state. This indicates that temperament is not necessarily unchangeable and unmodifiable in the way once supposed. Moreover the physical differences with which temperament is associated are those usually handed down by inheritance. In this way temperament may be regarded as hereditary.

But what is it that the parents hand down to their offspring? Few horse lovers and owners would, I think, hesitate to claim that they can tell a good deal about a horse's temperament from its immediate outward appearance, although when a number of different people are asked for the signs on which they base their judgments each will probably give a different answer. Some go by the look in the eye, others by the angle of the ears, and still others by the general stance. Some go by the colour and some by the shape. But first appearances can be very misleading, and an animal, whatever its colour or shape, may behave very differently in different circumstances. I have already quoted

187

some examples of this in the behaviour of Netta and Guss. Quinque and Septem provided a good illustration of the same point. Quinque and Septem were as different to look at and as different in their temperaments as it is possible to imagine.

Quinque, both in the stable or out in the field, was the most friendly, tractable creature it could be hoped to see. She enjoyed nothing more than to stand or lie with her head on a human shoulder, being patted or stroked. Nothing would upset her. Dogs could nibble at her heels, and flags could be waved round her ears without her flinching. In the same situation Septem, on the other hand, would back suspiciously away. He would investigate hands or pockets with only the tip of his nose protruding at the end of an outstretched neck, and his hind quarters would always be hunched ready to draw back at the first sign of an unexpected movement. Quinque would follow any human happily past any hazards and into any arena; Septem would be reluctant to follow anyone anywhere until quite sure that all was safe. Visitors to the farm would remark at once on Quinque's perfect suitability as a child's pony, but they would eye Septem with disapproval and often with disfavour.

Yet the moment they were saddled and bridled the rôles would be changed. Quinque, always ready for a gallop, would be fidgeting about on her toes ready to interpret the slightest movement in the saddle as a signal to leap forward, while Septem, sullen but placid, would stand without moving while small children hauled themselves laboriously up his sides. For despite his antagonism towards humans while he was in the field, he was quite unmoved by potentially frightening situations away from it. He hardly stirred when he first met a lorry, and after once investigating milk churns and pieces of paper by the roadside paid them little further attention. When we were short of horses for riding lessons I did not hesitate to put small children on Septem, and although he was then only three, the pony would follow along on the leading rein as calmly and gently as the most staid old hand. Quinque, on the other hand, could only be trusted with competent horsemen. It was not that she wished anybody any harm, or that she had the slightest desire to hurt them. It

188

was merely that she could not resist action whenever the opportunity for it arose. So long as she remembered what she was meant to do, and so long as the temptations to do otherwise were not too great, she would behave with perfect decorum, but excitement went to her head like wine. At the slightest excuse she would leap into the air and be off, and being extremely fast her mad scampers across the countryside could have been very frightening to an inexperienced rider. With Septem such dangers never arose. Slow and reluctant in all his movements, he was slow to get off the mark at any time; slow to calm but also slow to excite.

The look in a horse's eye is another sign which can be very misleading. It is often held that the presence of white indicates potential viciousness, but it must be remembered that any horse will show a certain amount of white when looking backwards. It is true that a continual tendency to look back probably signifies discomfort, reluctance and suspicion on the horse's part, and that these sensations create an urge to escape. But a young horse which is being made to go away from others for the first time will almost invariably look back longingly at those it is leaving and will show a good deal of white in the process. This does not necessarily mean that it is going to be bad, although it does indicate a situation which needs skilful and tactful handling. Fair Lady, the chestnut Anglo-Arab mare who came to Stones Farm to be schooled when she was rising three, was as gentle and amenable a little horse as it would be possible to find. She had no fear of any human, nor any desire to hurt them, but for several weeks when first handled she was very reluctant to leave her friends in the paddock. Every time an attempt was made to turn her away from them she would look back grudgingly exhibiting an expanse of white in her eye which might have made the superstitious quake. Never, however, did Fair Lady do anything bad or vicious, and when she finally came to realize that a circle round the field did not mean that she was being taken from her friends for ever the habit of rolling her eyes backwards was gradually discontinued.

However, that some idea about a horse's temperament

should be forthcoming from its physical appearance is only to be expected in the light of what is known in other creatures. The question is, what are the really important signs?

In the first place, there is the matter of physique or body-build, whose significance in the case of humans was found to be considerable. That the same is true to some

FIGURE 22
Examples of the body-builds which typically accompany different temperaments in Man: (a) the easy-going; (b) the nervous and apprehensive.
—And their equivalents in the horse world: (a) a Clydesdale; (b) an English thoroughbred.

extent in horses is, of course, well known. The different breeds not only have different conformations but also different mental tendencies. The English thoroughbred, with its long legs and slight body, is typically excitable, hypersensitive, nervous and fidgety (like the tall, thin, artistic human!), whereas the heavy Highland pony is more stolid and thoughtful. The Welsh cob, with its small head and fine legs is gay and mischievous in comparison with the well-rounded shire (see Fig. 22). But even among animals of the same breed and very similar conformation different degrees of these temperamental differences can be found. Not all thoroughbreds are equally nervous and excitable, nor all cobs equally placid.

It will probably be admitted by most people that among

190

all horses, as among most other animals, there are two definitely distinguishable types: the 'good-doers', who always look sleek, fat and round, and the 'bad-doers', who, whatever the breed and however much they are given to eat, always look angular and poor. That the differences between good- and bad-doers are also to some extent associated with differences of temperament is further recognized. The good-doers, like fat people, are usually of a fairly calm disposition. After being frightened or upset they regain their composure quickly. When returning to their boxes after a day's work they settle down at once to make themselves comfortable. The bad-doers, however, calm down more slowly, and on returning to their boxes after work will keep peering over their doors expectantly, breaking into a sweat, stamping and fretting. A mouthful of food is snatched occasionally, but remains unchewed in the corner of the mouth. If they have been ridden hard or frightened at any time they will always anticipate the worst. They are unable to throw off fear quickly or forget discomforts.

It even seems to be possible that the temperamental differences associated with appetite may counteract somewhat those due to inherited physique. Octavius was a typical bob-tailed cob, who, when he first came to Stones Farm after many months at grass, was as round as a barrel, with the thick neck and apple-like quarters characteristic of his type. It was obvious, however, from the moment he arrived, that Octavius was difficult to feed. For the whole of his first night he stood in his new stable with his head over the door, sweating and fretting, and did not touch a mouthful of the hay or water provided. Even later, when he settled down and got used to his new surroundings, his feeds were never eaten with gusto, and he was extremely difficult to keep in condition. By the middle of the hunting season his ribs were showing, his quarters were angular, and his back hollow.

Octavius showed as much of a bad-doer's temperament as a cob is probably ever capable of doing. Although he gave many children their first riding lessons and others their first canters off the leading rein; although he taught jumping better than any human instructor and would take a beginner out hunting like a nanny, the slightest rustle in the field, the slightest movement in the stable, or the sound of another animal in the far distance would put him on the alert at once. He was always gay, lively and active, fidgety and apprehensive. Perhaps it was just these cross-influences which made him the useful animal he was—a pony which would take small children for their first rides and yet at the same time give a 6 ft. man a good day's hunting.

Causes for the association between temperament and condition are not hard to find. In the first place, it is not always the sleek body which causes the peaceful mind, but rather the mind which influences the body. An animal that eats in peace gives its digestion every assistance and will be likely to put its food to the proper use. One that snatches at mouthfuls and eats while it rampages, cannot digest in the same way or store fat so well. But a simple and obvious explanation such as this cannot very well account for the temperamental differences associated with inherited body-build or conformation. Why should the thoroughbred be more nervous than the Highland cob? Why the Arab more spirited than the Dartmoor?

The reasons may be similar to those which account for the relationship between personality and body-build in humans.

A large horse with a heavy frame will, like a big man, need more to eat than a small, wiry individual. Its appetite will thus be correspondingly larger, and the dangers and threats it will be prepared to face in order to satisfy hunger will at the same time be greater. It will not hesitate to fight those who try to prevent it from eating, or kick at those who it thinks are likely to take its share of food. The lightly built horse, on the other hand, will seek rest and peace rather than food. Not only will it lack the fighting stamina of its sturdier mates, but it will concentrate on obtaining different things.

There is little doubt that habits set up in early youth, especially those associated with satisfying basic needs, are usually carried over into later life. A foal which is used to chasing its contemporaries away from the choicest tufts of grass when young will go on chasing them from mares when

192

older. It will quickly become a Billy Bunter—fat, assertive, domineering, yet possibly at the same time sensitive and suspicious. One that was constantly being chased by its contemporaries would forever be on the defensive, ready to flee and retreat, afraid the whole time that someone was after it; it would become a Unus, shy, retiring and submissive.

But to what extent are these patterns of behaviour acquired as a result of experience and how far are they inborn? There is little doubt that some behaviour patterns *are* inborn, and I have already quoted instances of quite idiosyncratic acts appearing in successive generations when the relevant stimulus was present. But in most aspects of behaviour, a distinction between the effects of heredity and environnment is almost impossible to make. The attitude of the dam plays a large rôle, but it is not the only one. Two of my own foals, Guss and Gracie, demonstrated this quite clearly. Both foals were by Gamesman, and both were out of thoroughbred mares. Gracie's dam, Late Coup, was twenty years old at the time, and was a great character, somewhat aloof and extremely aristocratic. Her manners were usually impeccable, but if one did by any chance cross her path, she showed her displeasure very clearly. For most of the time, she simply disdained human contact. Although Late Coup liked her food and stable in the Winter, catching her to put her into it was almost impossible. The gates had to be left open so that she could enter of her own accord.

Gracie, fortunately, shared none of this resentment. From the very first moment that she stood on her own four legs, she was far easier to catch and handle than her dam; and unlike her mother never lost an opportunity of being petted. There were many times when we had to lead Gracie into a stable or over a tricky piece of ground to show Late Coup the way.

The other foal, Guss, was the complete opposite. His dam, Whose Lady, was also a rather suspicious character but fortunately did not have Late Coup's mistrust of people. However, unlike Gracie, Guss treated people with dire suspicion. When submitting to being handled or groomed, he did so with all his limbs tensed for flight. Although he never

193

actually ran away when someone tried to catch him, he never came forward voluntarily. Had Guss been Late Coup's offspring and Gracie the daughter of Whose Lady, I would have been quite certain that these tendencies were copied or inherited from their respective dams.

The possibility that temperament is linked with pigmentation is another point which should be considered. It will be remembered that rats and mice of different colours were found to behave in different ways, and it has long been held by some people that the same is true of horses. Black horses have the reputation for being touchy and tending to rear. Chestnuts, like red-headed people, are said to be hot-tempered and are apt to pull. Greys are traditionally docile, tame and dependable, while bays have the reputation of being self-willed and mulish.

For many years I agreed with this, and thought that the differences in horses were probably accounted for by the distribution of sensory nerve-endings, which might vary with coat-colour. In some animal species there is no doubt that it does. Colour linked sensory deficiencies certainly do occur. Albinos, for instance, together with a deficiency of pigmentation in the skin, frequently have poorly developed eyes and ears, so that in general their senses of seeing and hearing are less effective than those of coloured animals. In the same way black rats, which were noted as being remarkably tame, were also found to have poor muscular development in general. This leads to slowness and loss of power in all their reactions, so that their apparent docility is probably only due to their inability to fight or escape as successfully as their fellows.

Generalising from these few examples, it seemed quite possible to me that differences in the distribution and development of various sense organs might accompany different coat-colours in horses and so account for some of the temperamental differences. The docile, insensitive grey, for instance, might not only lack pigmentation in its skin, but might also be deficient in touch spots there. It might literally not feel pricks and buffets as acutely as darker coloured individuals, except over its darker muzzle. On the other hand it might compensate for this deficiency by greater sensitivity to sight and sound—senses which would be more valuable to it in an undomesticated setting where, as has already been mentioned, its extreme visibility makes it vulnerable to enemies. Chestnuts, on the other hand, whose thin skin and fine hair provide little protection to the nerve endings on the surface of the body, could be more sensitive to touch stimuli than others. This would account for their tendency to respond readily to the slightest pressure on flanks and back, and for their apparent hot-headedness. Since chestnuts frequently have white mouths, the insensitivity to the bit could be accounted for on the same basis as that of the flanks in a grey horse.

These differences may still occur, but judging from my experiences with Nuki and her various descendents, they cannot account for all the differences of behaviour which one sees. Nuki's first two offspring, Nauri and Gamesman, were both greys, but were very different in temperament. Nauri was like Quinque, quick but loving; Gamesman was like Septem, slow but dependable. But Nuki has also produced bays and browns among her offspring, and I must confess that I have not noted any tendencies in her greys which were not present in at least one of the darker coloured children and vice versa.

CHAPTER VI

COMPLEXES AND VICES

In the previous chapters only those individual differences were considered which distinguish one normal aspect of behaviour from another. Besides these minor idiosyncrasies and characteristics, however, there exist more troublesome deviations of behaviour which are commonly known by the damning name of vices.

The causes of these vices and the ways in which they may be dealt with are matters which have been the subject of innumerable tirades and publications. There is hardly a book on horses which does not contain some reference to their origins and some suggestions as to their treatment; hardly a person who does not hold an opinion on the matter, nor one who would not thrust his opinion on to others. Being no exception to the general run of mankind, I cannot refrain from saying my own word on the subject, but I will try to approach the question from considering the nature and origin of behaviour difficulties in general.

In the first place, it is as well to make quite clear what is meant by a behaviour difficulty or an abnormality. There are various ways of defining it, but the outstanding features seem to be that the individuals in question are unable to adapt themselves normally to their environment. They are unable to live at peace with themselves or others, to make the most of their opportunities and to satisfy their basic needs and appetites. Because animals in these conditions show many of the characteristics of human beings suffering from mental or nervous breakdowns, they are often said to be 'neurotic' too.

196

The activities which indicate a neurosis may take various forms. In the first place, there may be signs of physical stress, such as sweating, shivering, rolling of the eyes, and salivating. In the second place there may be abnormalities of appetite such as the animal going off its food and drink, being unable to rest, or tending to attack others with which it was previously friendly. In the third place, there may be marked signs of restlessness and agitation, or their very opposites, complete immobility. In the fourth place there may be defects of perception: the animal fails to see or hear in the normal manner and tends to bump into obstacles so as to cause itself bodily harm. In the fifth place, the animal may develop stupid and stereotyped habits, such as licking the lips, swaying on the feet, stamping the ground or pacing up and down and round in circles.

PRECIPITATING CAUSES

The events or situations likely to precipitate breakdowns of this sort have been studied by a great many different workers and in a number of different animal species.

Conflict

In one important group of situations the animal appears to be in a state of unresolvable mental conflict due to the presence of two opposing urges, both equally strong. It does not know whether to come or go, to approach or avoid, to take or to reject. Professor Masserman studied the effect of such conflicts in cats.[28] Ordinary cats were put into a small cage and at a given signal—such as the ringing of a bell—were taught to take food from a little trough. The cats learned this easily, and after doing so would enter the cage where the training had been carried out willingly and contentedly. They would walk about it calmly while waiting for the signal, purring and rubbing themselves against their attendants. They showed, in fact, all the usual reactions of a normal, happy cat, but were alert all the time for the signal which would indicate food and pounced on the trough the moment this appeared. As soon as they had been thoroughly accustomed to their life in this environment, a new situation was introduced. After the signal, and as soon as the cats approached the food, a puff of air would be blown from the trough into their faces, making them start back unhappily. The cats were now in a serious quandary, caught between the desires to approach and to avoid, between the hunger which prompted them to go towards the food and the fear which prompted them to run away from it. Very soon they began to show many of the abnormalities of behaviour listed above. Instead of entering the test cage willingly and calmly, they fought to avoid being put into it at all. Instead of sitting quietly inside it, waiting for the signal, they paced up and down or lay immobile on the floor, as if unable to move at all. Occasionally some would resort to frantic and quite unnecessary stereotyped movements, such as licking their fur or scratching at the sides of the cage. At the sight of their attendants or of another cat with which they had previously been friendly their hackles would rise and they would prepare themselves for unprovoked and unaccustomed battle. All food, even that presented to them outside the test cage, was treated with suspicion and hostility, and as they became ever hungrier, so their agitation and abnormality increased. These reactions tended to persist long after the cats had been taken from the test cage, and could be seen in a variety of different surroundings.

Uncertainty

Another type of situation which produces the same sort of reaction is one in which an animal is faced with a problem beyond its powers of resolution. A dog can be trained to make one sort of response when it sees a circle and another when it sees an oval. Once the dog has learned these distinctions, the circle can be replaced by a slightly more elliptical shape and the oval by a slightly more circular one. The dog goes on making the 'circle' response to the more circular shape and the 'oval' response to the more oval shape. But when the two signs are made so nearly alike that the dog cannot distinguish them apart, then its whole behaviour begins to change. Instead of looking at the signs intelligently and voluntarily, it will try to escape from the whole

198

situation. Like Masserman's cats, it will go off its food, will take to panting or snapping at everything within reach, will give up and appear unable to move or will charge about, jumping at the slightest sounds.

Professor Pavlov found much the same behaviour in his dogs which, because of perceptual difficulties, were uncertain of their future. Some of his dogs were rewarded with food every time they saw one shape and received a small electric shock every time they saw another. As long as the shapes and signals were quite distinct, so that the animals knew what to expect after each one, they remained perfectly calm and unmoved. They would wag their tails at the expectation of food, and brace themselves for the minor unpleasantness of the shock. But when the two signals became so nearly alike that the dogs could not tell them apart and never knew whether to expect food or shock, then they began to show the typical signs of complete and lasting mental breakdown.

That it cannot have been the pain of the shock alone which affected Pavlov's animals and caused this state is clear from the fact that during the early trials the dogs showed little discomfort or displeasure, even in the face of fairly strong currents. But another series of experiments carried out on sheep points to the same conclusion even more strongly. Two sheep which had been notable previously for their stable and intelligent behaviour were trained to expect a small electric shock every time they heard a certain bell. They picked up this association quite quickly and showed little disturbance or discomfort in the process.[25] The experimenter then tried to see if they could learn to expect the shock after every other signal only, and consequently he shocked the animal only after alternate signals. Despite the fact that the sheep were now only receiving half the original number of shocks, they appeared far more unhappy, bewildered and perplexed than before. Unable to 'learn' the rule involved, they became permanently apprehensive, timid, seclusive and unsettled, and finally had to be abandoned as laboratory 'guinea-pigs'.

Restriction
Animals do not necessarily and inevitably show the com-

199

pletely catastrophic breakdown described above in situations which they cannot solve. Sometimes they build up a kind of mental defence by developing one fixed pattern of reaction to which they resort every time they are in doubt. A pig which was being trained to differentiate between two bells of a different pitch, one of which was followed by food and the other by a shock, avoided having to make the mental effort of deciding which to expect by rushing to its trough after every signal it received. When the edge of its trough was electrified so that after the wrong signals it received a shock from this as well, it found another way out of its dilemma by stamping with its feet every time it heard a bell and refusing to go near its trough at all. Only when it was closely confined in a tight harness so that all escaping movements were prevented and it was forced to face the issue did it really break down and become neurotic.

Rats seem especially prone to develop stereotyped habits of the sort adopted by this pig. If carefully handled, they can learn to differentiate between very complex perceptual patterns, but if their training is hurried or if they are introduced to too many different tasks at once, they will adopt rigid habits in self-defence which are difficult to eradicate later on. Horses show the same tendency. Tertia's habit of kicking out sideways when asked to lead with the off-fore at a canter was a case in point.

It may be wondered what all these stories have to do with vices and why they are being reported in such detail here. The reason is that many of the activities recognized as vices in horses—such as rearing, biting, bucking, kicking, weaving (a state in which the animal sways to and fro on its feet in the stable), and wind-sucking—appear when carefully analysed to have much in common with the stereotyped habits seen in neurotic animals. Like the latter, they are not only purposeless and compulsive, but are associated with a particular state of mind. The vicious horse, like the neurotic cat or sheep, is seldom contented. He is restless, agitated and unhappy. Moreover, the habits he develops, once they are established, persist long after he has been removed from the scene or incident by which they were first aroused and may remain as a life-long affliction. It seems more than likely, therefore, that viciousness is a symptom of a mental breakdown in a horse—of a neurosis—and that it may be caused by the same kind of situations which causes these in other animals. The nature of neuroses and the ways in which they may be treated are therefore matters of prime concern to anyone dealing with vices in horses.

PREDISPOSITION

The sorts of situation likely to precipitate a mental break-down have just been described, but although *all* animals may break down if they are subjected to sufficiently great strains or stresses for a sufficiently long time, not all do so equally quickly or remain disturbed for an equally long time. One dog may become quite hysterical after a short period in a situation of uncertainty and may remain suspicious and hostile for the rest of its life. Another will stand up to the strain for several hours before showing signs of discomfort, and even then will recover its previous composure quickly after release. What factors cause the differences between these types, making the one basically neurotic while the other escapes? This is an important question and one to which a great deal of thought and attention have been devoted.

Heredity
One factor which seems to play an important part in causing this distinction is heredity. An animal which is inclined to be easily upset will pass on this tendency to its off-spring, and by selective breeding it is possible to produce strains of rats or mice which are quite distinct from one another in their ability to withstand stresses. However, a curious fact has been noted from these experiments—namely, that animals which are extremely sensitive to and liable to break down in one situation may not show any abnormal sensitivity in others. By selective breeding it is not possible to produce animals of a generally neurotic disposition, only those with a tendency to break down in the same circumstances as their parents. For this reason it is suspected, although not yet fully

201

established, that the liability to breakdown lies in congenital weaknesses of some aspect of the physical equipment, such as in the glandular system, the central nervous system, or in the senses. Thus, an animal which tends to have epileptic fits when faced with the problem of discriminating between different sounds may have some weakness of its hearing; one which breaks down in a task involving visual discrimination may have a weakness in its eyes.

In horses, the same factors may operate. The tendency for Samantha's first two foals to have 'inherited' her tendency to weave has already been mentioned. This did not make them either more nervous or more difficult to manage in other situations, which suggests that it was something specific to standing about idly in the stable which their constitutions could not cope with.

Physical Condition

Another factor influencing the liability to breakdown is the physical condition of the body at the time the animal is subjected to stress. If it is suffering from the after-effects of an illness, if it is very tired, on a diet too rich or too poor for it, or if for any other reason it is lacking in condition, an animal is much more liable to give in and become confused or neurotic than otherwise. Although the abnormalities which occur under these conditions will often disappear when the animal is back in full health, it is always possible that the habits of behaviour established at this time may persist and become fixed and permanent.

Deprivation during Development

As has been mentioned in a previous chapter, an individual's mental development passes through various phases, and during each of these phases it is important that certain basic needs should be satisfied. If such satisfaction is not forth-coming at the right time, the animal seems to harbour a permanent lack or deficit which places it under a continual mental strain throughout later life. Although it may be able to adjust itself to the demands of a simple environment without showing any sign of abnormality, any great stress in

202

the form of conflict or uncertainty will be quite sufficient to precipitate a general breakdown.

Among horses it is possible that each of the above factors plays some part in causing a vice to be established. Probably, if looked for hard enough, both a precipitating cause—i.e., some situation of conflict, uncertainty or frustration—as well as an underlying disposition could be found in every case. But as in humans, each case would probably have to be considered individually to be fully understood. A condition which upsets one person leaves another unmoved; circumstances sufficient to send one child mad leave another merely irritated. Horses have almost as wide a variety of likes, needs, and tendencies as human beings. To generalize from one case about others would almost certainly be most misleading.

TREATMENT

Even when the cause of a mental breakdown is known, its cure is not bound to follow. The treatment of mental illness is a very difficult problem, and a very different one from that of physical ailments. When a person is bodily sick, the procedure is fairly straight-forward. If the cause can be counteracted, the patient can usually be restored to health fairly easily. A physical deficiency is supplemented or an infection removed, and all is well.

But a mental event cannot be removed like a septic appendix or destroyed like an unwanted microbe. Nor can it be washed away like a poison. A mental event, once it has been experienced, is ineradicable. Hence, the only way in which a conflict or a habit can be dealt with is by building more experiences on top of it to counteract it. A journey abroad or a period of rest in a hospital or nursing-home were the procedures which used to be recommended. While in these new surroundings the patients were urged to think about new things. They were trained in new occupations, and their morale was boosted by encouragement and reassurance. Such treatment is often successful in that the patient seems to get over his trouble and appears fit to lead a normal, useful life, but it is often, unfortunately, found that a return to the previous environment and situation will precipitate a recurrence of the neurosis no less incapacitating than its first appearance.

If new habits or new attitudes are built up systematically, using all that is known about learning to ensure that they stick, the results are more satisfactory. 'Behaviour Therapy' has now become a recognised and widely practiced form of treatment, claiming many successes in all types of patient.[43]

Rest and retraining have been tried on neurotic animals as well as humans. Pavlov and Masserman kept special country houses for the reception and treatment of animal patients, but when the animals were returned to the situations where the neurosis originally developed the old behaviour was often found to return as well.

One of the sheep which broke down when being trained to the sound of a bell was given five years rest in new surroundings and seemed to have recovered completely. Yet when taken back to the laboratory in which its neurosis had developed it showed the same symptoms as on the first occasion. Treatment by physical methods is also useful and effective in some cases, although its value is limited in animals as it is in man. A series of electric shocks so strong that they cause the animal to lose consciousness may temporarily cure a rat of neurotic behaviour, but leaves it incapable for some time of learning anything new. As the latter defect clears up, so the tendencies towards neurosis return. Some brain operations are extremely successful on monkeys (indeed it was the amazing 'cure' produced in a neurotic chimpanzee by one such operation which prompted the original use of this technique in humans); but they seem to leave the subjects indisputably altered. The operated apes cease to show a healthy fear of the most obvious dangers; they no longer want to hunt or fight, but lie around eating and growing fat.

There appear, in fact, to be no short cuts to victory over a nervous breakdown, and no single method can be advocated as a cure for all. The pros and cons of different methods of treatment must be weighed up carefully in each individual situation and balanced against the desired end. Above all it is now realised that as much attention must be given to the conditions to which an individual is returned after treatment as to the condition of the individual himself.

This last fact, however, gives a clue to the best way of treating horses, for although manipulation of and alterations to the environment present many problems where human beings are concerned, they are not usually difficult in the case of animals. It is seldom impossible to remove a horse from an environment where a vice was precipitated, and to retrain it till its habits are altered. What *is* difficult is to return the animal to the same situation as it was in before without the old habits reappearing. But why should it be returned? Once the animal's basic disposition, its abilities and potentialities have been totted up, is it not best to put it in an environment where these deficiencies will not matter?

There is a tendency among modern psychologists to place the onus for all the misdemeanours of the individual on the society which produced him. If a child kills or steals, it is his parents who get the blame, not him. If a youth arms himself and attacks old women, fault is found with the films and books he has been allowed to see. Although this may appear at first sight almost too easy a way out, it cannot be denied that the attitudes of those in authority are usually reflected in the behaviour of subordinates. In the same way, if a horse exhibits bad habits, these are an indication that it is being either badly ridden or badly looked after. It will be useless in such instances to try to cure the horse; it is mainly in an attempt to try to cure the keepers of horses through increasing their insight into the nature of their animals that this book has been written.

REFERENCES

1. Annette, M. 1972. *The distribution of manual asymmetry*, Brit. J. Psychol., *63*, 343.
2. Archer, M. 1973. *The Species Preferences of Grazing Horses*, J. Br. Grassld. Soc., *28*, 123.
3. Barrett, S.A. 1967. *Instinct and Intelligence*, Macgibbon & Kee, London.
4. Bartlett, F.C. 1932. *Remembering*, Cambridge University Press.
5. Bindra, D. 1970. *Emotion and Behaviour Theory*, Ch. 1 in Physiology Correlates of Emotion. Ed. P. Black, Academic Press.
6. Blandingen, W. 1972. *Psychologie und Verhastenwerde des Pferdes*, Erich Hoffnen Verlag.
7. Boring, E.G., Langfield, H.S., & Weld, H.P. 1948. *Foundations of Experimental Psychology*, Wiley & Sons, N.Y.
8. Fox, H.M. 1940. *The Personality of Animals*, Penguin Books.
9. Goldschmidt, V. 1972. *Social Behaviour in Camargue horses*, Proc. Soc. Ethol. & Ecol. of Dom. Ams, Freiburg a.B.
10. Grzimek, B. 1949. *Right-Left handedness in Horses*, Z. Tierpsych, 7. 1406.
11. Grzimek, B. 1952. *Colour Vision of Horses*, Z. Tierpsychol, 11, 23.
12. Harlow, H.F. and M.K. 1970. *Development aspects of Soc. Behaviour*, Ch. 3 in Physiological Correlates of Emotion. Ed. P. Black, Academic Press.
13. Hebb, D.O. 1946. *On the Nature of Fear*, Psychol. Rev., *53*, 259.
14. Hebb, D.O. 1949. *Organization of Behaviour*, John Wiley & Sons.
15. Hediger, H. 1955. *The Behaviour of Animals in Zoos and Circuses*, Butterworths.
16. Heim, A. 1970. *Intelligence and Personality*, Penguin Books.

17. Hinde, R.A., & Hinde, J.S. 1973. *Constraints of Learning*, Academic Press.
18. Humphrey, G. 1933. *The Nature of Learning*, Kegan Paul & Co.
19. Katz, D. 1927. *Animals and Men*, Longmans Green, London.
20. Keeler, C.E. 1947. *Coat-Colour and Temperament*, J. Hered, *38*, 271.
21. Kiley, M. 1972. *The Vocalization of Ungulates*, Z. Tierpsychol, *31*, 171.
22. Klingel, H. 1965. *Notes on the biology of Plains Zebras*, E. African Wildlife Journal, *3*, 86.
23. Köhler, I. 1962. *Experiments with Goggles*, Sci. *206*, 62.
24. Kretschmer, E. 1925. *Physique and Character*, Harcourt Brace, N. York.
25. Liddell, H.S. 1938. *Experiments, neuroses and mental disorder*, Am. J. Psychiat. *94*, 1035.
26. Lorenz, K. 1952. *King Solomon's Ring*, Methuen & Co.
27. Lorenz, K. 1966. *Evaluation and Modification of Behaviour*, Methuen & Co.
28. Masserman, J.H. 1943. *Behaviour and Neuroses*, University Chicago Press.
29. Montgomery, G.G. 1957. *Sociality of the Domestic Horse*, Trans. Kansas Acad. Sci. *60*, 419.
30. Ödberg, F. 1972. *Acoustic Expression in Horses*, Proc. Soc. of Vet. Ethol. & Ecol. Freiburg a.B.
31. Ödberg, F. 1972. *Eliminative Behaviour and Paddock Management*, Equine Behav. *1*, 5.
32. Pavlov, I.P. 1927. *Conditioned Reflexes*, Oxford University Press.
33. Ricard, M. 1969. *The Mystery of Animal Migration*, Constable & Co., London.
34. Rossdale, R.P. 1968. *Perinatal Behaviour of the TB Horse*, Brit. Vet. J. *124*, 540.
35. Tinbergen, N. 1953. *Social Behaviour in Animals*, Methuen & Co.
36. Thorndike, E.L. 1911. *Animal Intelligences*, Macmillan & Co.
37. Tyler, S.J. 1972. *The Behaviour and Social Organization of New Forest Ponies*, An. Behav. Monog. *5*, Part 2.
38. von Frisch, K. 1954. *The Dancing Bees*, Methuen & Co.
39. Walls, G.L. 1942. *The Vertebrate Eye*, Cranbrook Inst. Sci. Bull. No. 19.
40. Waring, G. 1971. *Sounds of the Horse*, Proc. Ecol. Soc. Am. Colorado.

41. Waring, G. 1972. *Socialization and Development in Newborn horses*, Proc. Ethology & Ecology of Dom. Ams. Freiburg. a.B.

42. Welch, R.M. & Stratford, S.M. 1972. *The Herd and the Bell Mare*, Equine Behav. *1*, 20.

43. Wolpe, J. 1958. *Psychotherapy by reciprocal inhibition*, Stanford University Press. California.

44. Woodhouse, B. 1954. *Talking to Animals*, Faber & Faber, London.

45. Williams, M. 1960. *Adventures Unbridled*, Methuen & Co. (Currently reprinting in America under the title *Training A Horse Without Bit or Bridle*, A.S. Barnes). Publication due 1976.

46. Williams, M. 1971. *A Breed of Horses*, Methuen & Co.

47. Williams, M. 1971. *Brain Damage and the Mind*, Penguin Books.

48. Williams, M. 1972. *Laterality and Suckling in foals*, Proc. Soc. Ethol. & Ecol. Dom. Ams. Freiburg a.B.

49. Williams, M. 1973. *Artificial Rearing and the Social Behaviour of Foals*, Eq. Vet. J. *6*.

50. Zangwill, O.L. 1963. *The cerebral localization of Function*, Advance Sci. Vol. *20*, 1.

51. Zuckerman, S. 1932. *The Social Life of Monkeys and Apes*, Kegan Paul & Co.